BERNINI
THE SCULPTURES

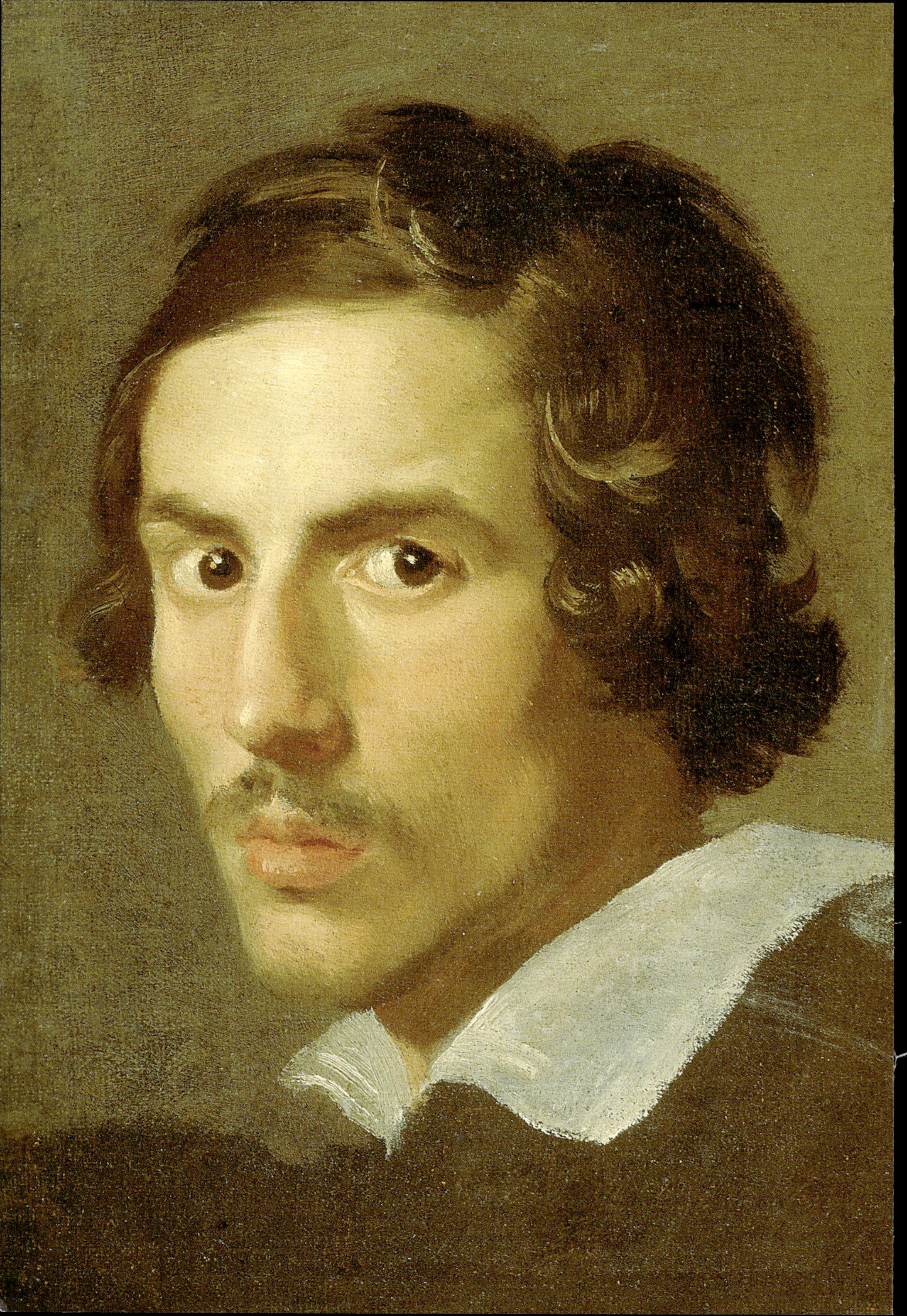

BERNINI

THE SCULPTURES Maria Grazia Bernardini

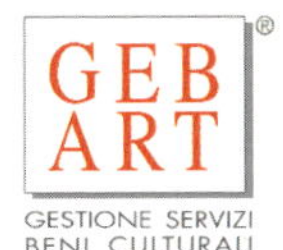

Via Prenestina 685 - 00155 Roma
info@gebart.it - www.gebart.it

ISBN 978-88-98302-01-7

Printed in Italy
Reprints: 2013, 2014

Editor-in-chief and picture research

Stefania Spirito

Graphic design

BerardiDesignTeam

Translation

Oona Maria Smyth

Photolithography and printing

Miligraf S.r.l., Rome

Facing title-page:
G. L. Bernini, *Self-Portrait as a Young Man* (c. 1623), Rome, Galleria Borghese.

CONTENT

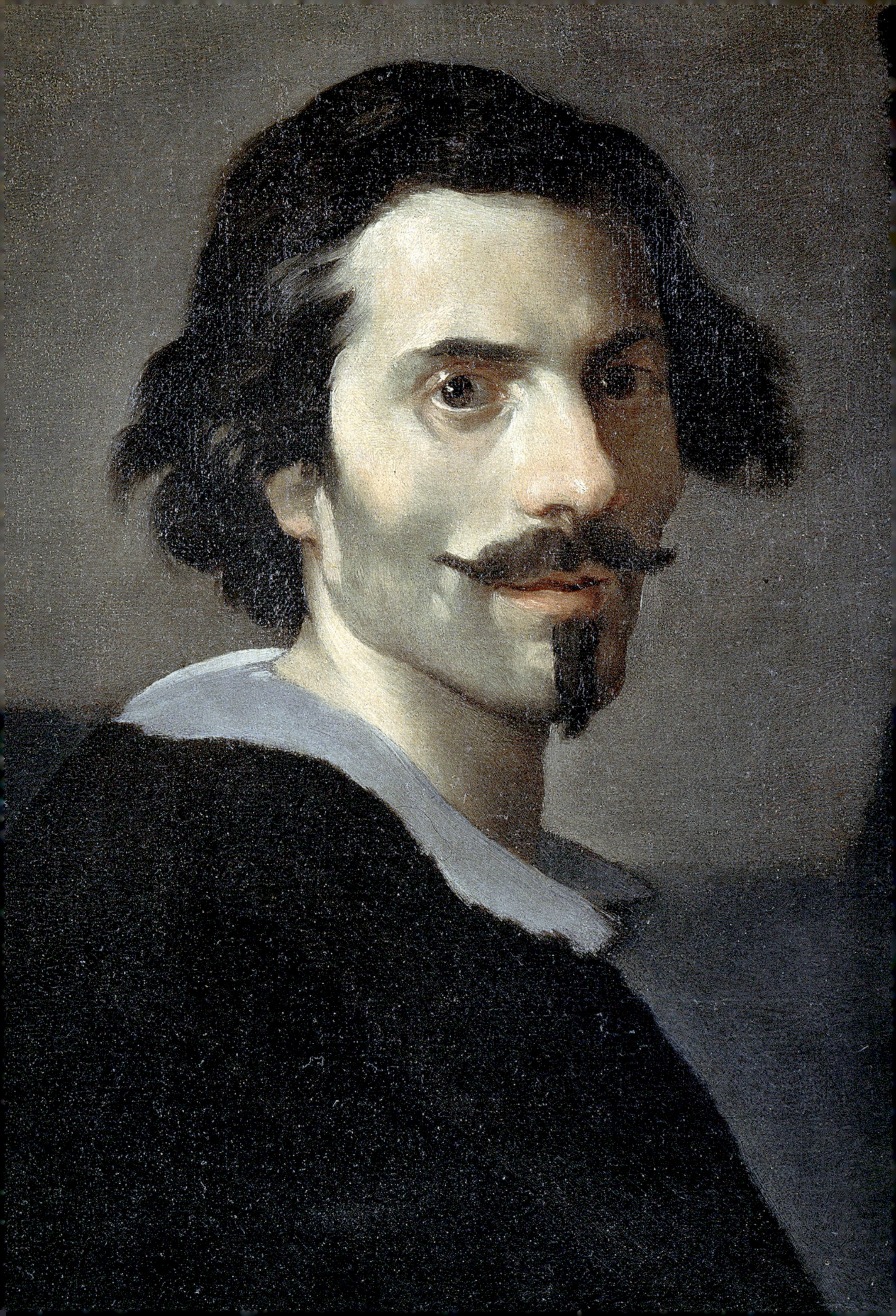

INTRODUCTION

Although 16th-century art in Rome is mainly linked to the great cycles of paintings in the Sistine Chapel by Michelangelo, in Raphael's Stanze, in the Vatican Gallery of Maps, and the ambitious projects of Sixtus V, in the 17th century it was prevalently represented by sculpture: chapels, altars, altarpieces, marble statue groups, figures of saints or allegorical characters, funerary monuments and decorative elements proliferated and spread throughout sacred buildings; fountains and obelisks embellished squares and streets; statues, coats of arms, cartouches and monumental doorways animated the façades of churches and palaces; portrait busts filled the private galleries of the nobility.

The sheer scale of Bernini's works, which can be found in every corner of the city, along with the absolute originality of his inventions, which opened a new phase in the history of art, mean that no study of Baroque sculpture in Rome can be considered complete without an illustration of his creations. Bernini (Fig. 1) was not only a sculptor, he was also an architect, painter, town-planner, draughtsman, engraver, playwright and scenographer. With his outstanding creative powers, multifaceted genius, exceptional abilities as an organiser of colossal events and exuberant personality, he monopolised most of Rome's major artistic projects, causing Passeri to describe him as "that dragon who ceaselessly guards the gardens of the Hesperides, making sure no one else should snatch the golden apples of papal favour, spitting poison everywhere and planting ferocious thorns of loathing along the path that led to rich rewards". A recent exhibition rightly termed him the "director of the baroque".

His art has left a lasting mark on the way Rome presents itself, shaping its *forma urbis*. Next to him, the figures of great sculptors like Algardi and Duquesnoy, both creators of superb masterpieces, pale in comparison. The correspondence between Francesco I, Duke of Modena, and his brother, a cardinal who was in Rome at the time, provides an idea of the enormous prestige and power enjoyed by Bernini. As Cardinal Rinaldi wrote to Francesco, who wished to have his bust portrayed: "Bernini works only as a favour to friends or at the request of important personages. With him, one cannot fix in advance either a schedule or a price. [...] For marble portraits, whether busts or half figures, Algardi the sculptor demands one hundred and fifty *scudi* plus the marble [...] and will deliver the work in one and half months. (Letter of 16 July 1650, ASM).

Fig. 1
G. L. Bernini,
Self-Portrait as a Mature Man (c. 1635), Rome,
Galleria Borghese.

THE FORMATIVE YEARS

Gian Lorenzo Bernini came to Rome aged around seven in 1606. He was born in Naples in 1598 to Pietro Bernini, a Tuscan sculptor who moved there in 1584 before being called to Rome by Pope Paul V. As a boy, Bernini worked alongside his father in two of the largest and most prestigious sculptural undertakings of the first two decades of the century: the Pauline Chapel in the Basilica of Santa Maria Maggiore (1605-1611) on behalf of Pope Paul V, and the Barberini Chapel in the church of Sant'Andrea della Valle (1604-1618) for the Pronotary Apostolic Francesco Barberini commissioned by Cardinal Maffeo Barberini, future Pope Urban VIII, which saw Pietro Bernini flanked by the leading sculptors of the time. They included an extremely young Gian Lorenzo, who sculpted two small angels in the Barberini Chapel (Fig. 2).

The sculptures in these two projects show the first signs that the late Mannerist style is making way for the vigour and naturalism typical of the Baroque language. In the episode of the *Coronation of Clement VIII* and in the *Caryatids* in the Pauline Chapel, in the relief with the *Assumption* (now in the baptistery of the basilica, but originally intended for the entrance wall to the chapel) Pietro's style is characterised by a search for decorative effects obtained by extensive use of the drill in locks of hair or beards, by an incredible technical virtuosity revealed in the sharp angular folds, by an extremely animated and crowded composition, and, above all, by pictorial effects obtained by means of continuous passages from high to low relief creating strong chiaroscuro effects. In the sculpture depicting *St John the Baptist* in the Barberini Chapel, Pietro eschews the rigidly static position typical of a statue for an undefined pose of the figure, which, as has been pointed out, may be seated or about to rise. In the *St Martha* (Fig. 3) – also in the Barberini Chapel – Francesco Mochi, one of the great artists of the first half of the century, pursues a naturalism and narrative aims that were wholly new and that would be taken up by the young Gian Lorenzo when carving his future Borghese sculptures: the saint is shown bending forward with holy water to tame the dragon who is grasping

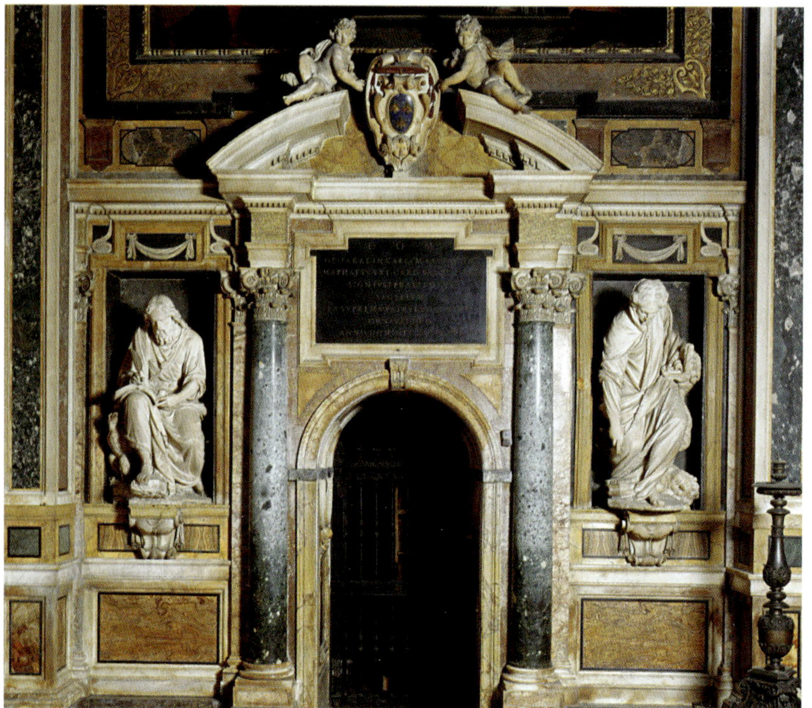

Fig. 2 (left)
Barberini Chapel (1604-18), right wall, Rome, Church of Sant'Andrea della Valle.

Fig. 3 (right)
Francesco Mochi, *St Martha* (1609-17), Rome, Church of Sant'Andrea della Valle, Barberini Chapel.

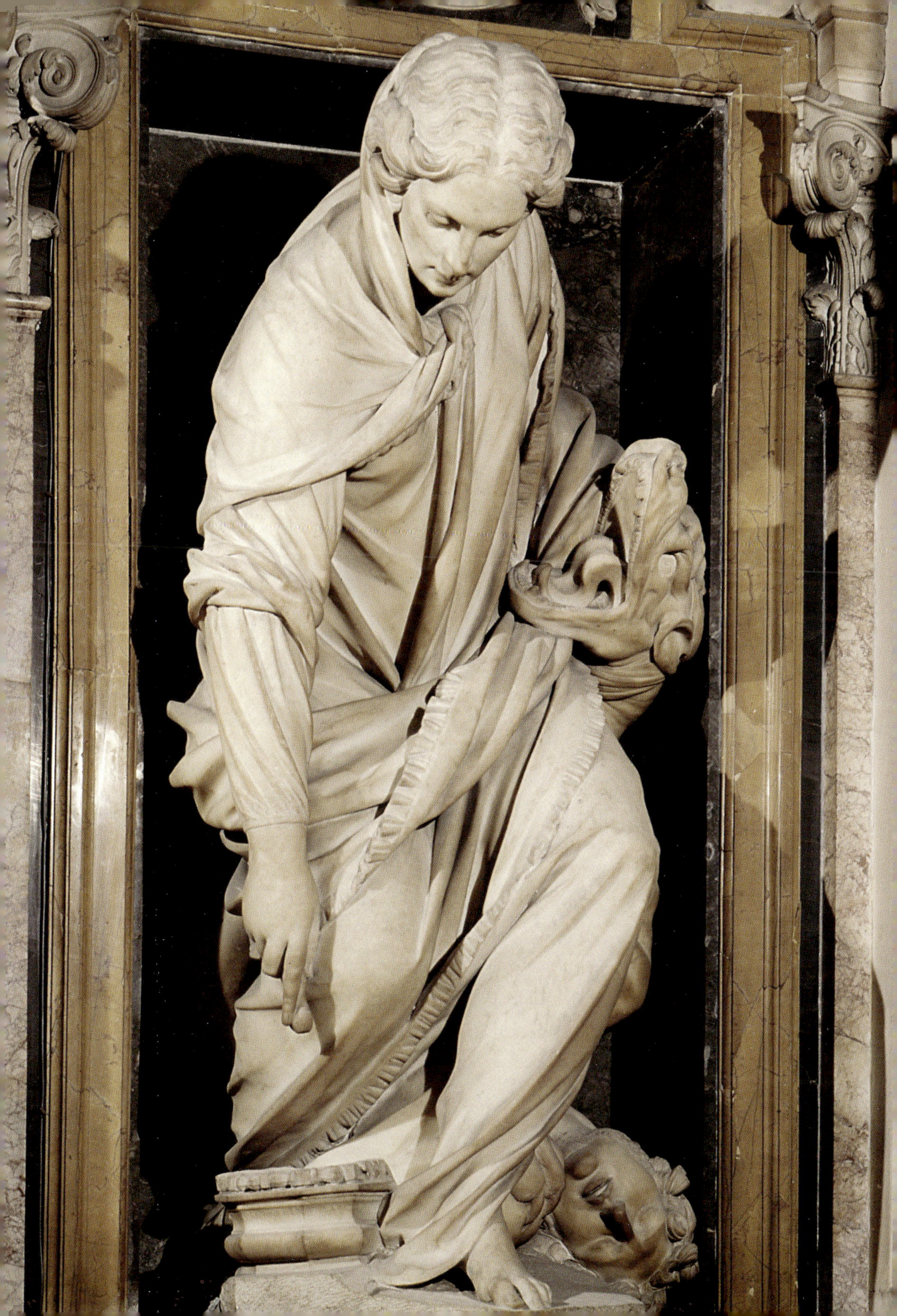

a youth in his claws. Bernini obviously spent his time in his father's workshop observing and learning, but he also studied classical sculpture. According to his biographers the young artist would leave Santa Maria Maggiore every morning to go to the Vatican palaces, where he would study the legacy of antique art. His particular fascination with the sculptures of *Antinous* and the *Belvedere Apollo* (Fig. 4) would emerge with great clarity in his subsequent works.

In the Vatican palaces the young Bernini could linger before the works of Michelangelo and Raphael who had always been considered the supreme masters, and, as an acute observer, he also looked to the art being painted in his own period, in particular by the Bolognese artists, Annibale Carracci, Guido Reni, and Giovanni Lanfranco, who had painted such extraordinary works between the late 16th century and early 17th century, like the Farnese Gallery, the *Aurora* in the Casino Pallavicini, the Annunziata Chapel in the Quirinal palace, as well as by Caravaggio and Rubens.

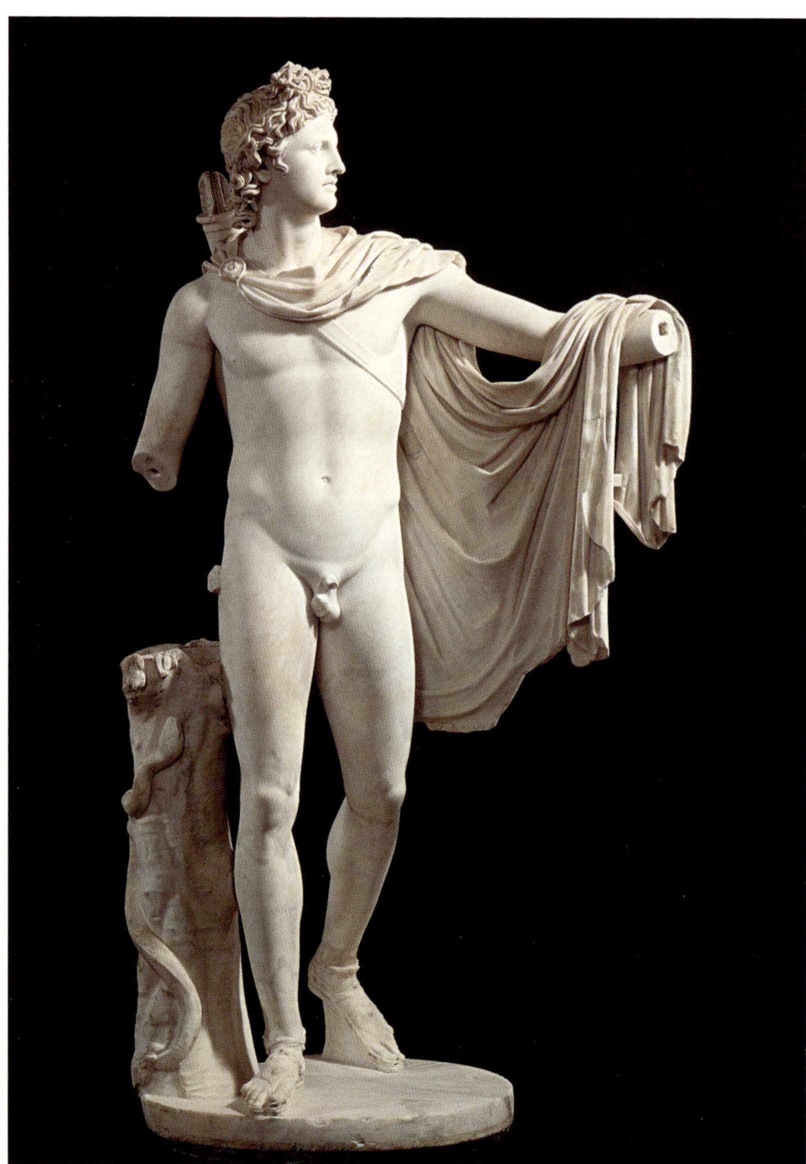

Fig. 4 (left)
Belvedere Apollo
(c. 350 BC),
Musei Vaticani.

Fig. 5 (right)
G. L. Bernini,
Goat Amalthea
(before 1615), Rome,
Galleria Borghese.

THE YOUTHFUL WORKS

Bernini was an *enfant prodige* who began to work with his father from an early age; most astonishingly, he executed his first own pieces at the age of just ten or twelve. His *Goat Amalthea*, a small sculpture group dating to before 1615 or possibly even to 1609 (Fig. 5-6; Rome, Galleria Borghese), reveals the impact of his innovations on formal, technical as well as conceptual levels in its playful depiction of a scene showing the infant Jupiter jesting with the goat who was his wet-nurse, its search for naturalism in the figures, and its tactile handling, verging on the chromatic, of the marble obtained by using different carving techniques according to the material involved – whether the fleece of the goat, the tender skin of the infant or the milk in the bowl.

A few years later, between 1616 and 1618, when Bernini was still a boy, he executed a vast number of sculptures, which can be already be considered true masterpieces: the *St Lawrence* (Florence, Galleria degli Uffizi), which betrays a debt towards the figure of *Adam* by Michelangelo, the *St Sebastian* (Madrid, Museo Thyssen-Bornemisza) which expresses the saint's state of abandonment with an unusual intensity, the *Satyr* (New York, Metropolitan

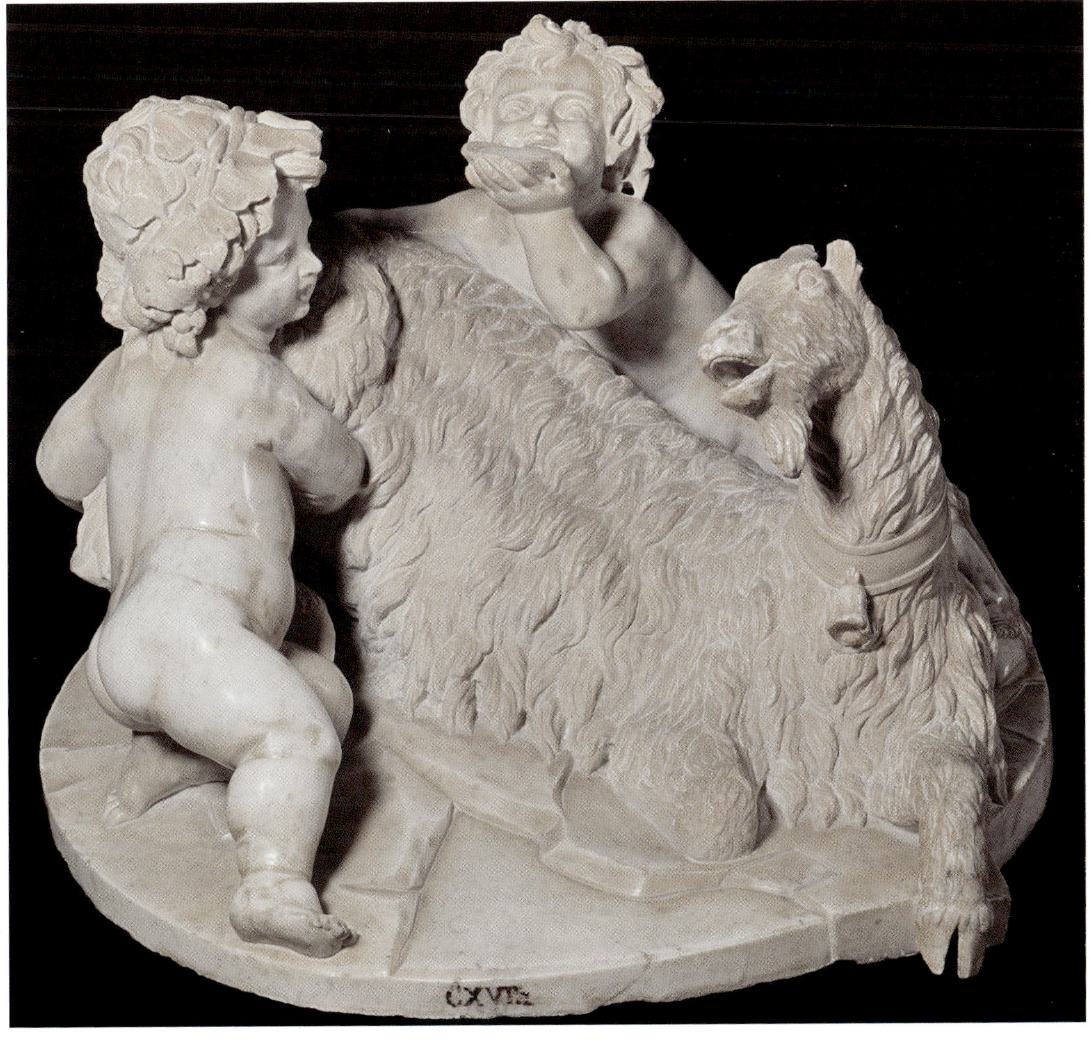

Museum of Art) and the *Putto on a Dolphin* (Berlin, Staatliche Museen), where the artist reveals his extraordinary technical skills and ability to represent movement. These works were joined by portraits, a genre in which he would become the leading artist of his period, in demand by the mighty of the earth, popes, kings, princes and cardinals. His *Portrait of Paul V* (Fig. 7; Rome, Galleria Borghese), a bust whose small dimensions belie its great expressive intensity and formal sophistication, reveals his approach, which is characterised by his detailed rendering of the surface of the marble, sculpted using different techniques depending on the material involved, thus causing the sculpture to appear natural and alive. Observers examining this small sculpture are fascinated by the rich details (the embroidered gown, shirt, jewel, face, beard and hair) and the white marble, which appears to exhibit varying hues.

In 1618 he received the most prestigious commission to which a young artist could possibly aspire: the nephew of Paul V, the powerful cardinal Scipione Borghese, commissioned him to carry out three large sculpture groups (a fourth one would be added soon after) for his personal villa. In the space of only a few years, Bernini rose dramatically to fame, seizing centre stage and revolutionising the way sculpture was conceived.

The first group, which has a complex composition, depicts *Aeneas, Anchises and Ascanius Fleeing Troy* by means of three characters alluding to the three ages of man: Aeneas, who is carrying his father Anchises on his shoulders and holding the hand of his son, Ascanius, is fleeing Troy. Although the masterly pose of Aeneas, the extensive drillwork and depiction of a self-contained story all reveal his debt to his father along with lingering Mannerist influences, the innovations of Bernini's art are equally evident. He reveals great awareness in his handling of the marble surface along with an extraordinary capacity to represent the emotions, affections, and melancholy of his subjects, as well as the effort being sustained by Aeneas and the fear gripping his young son.

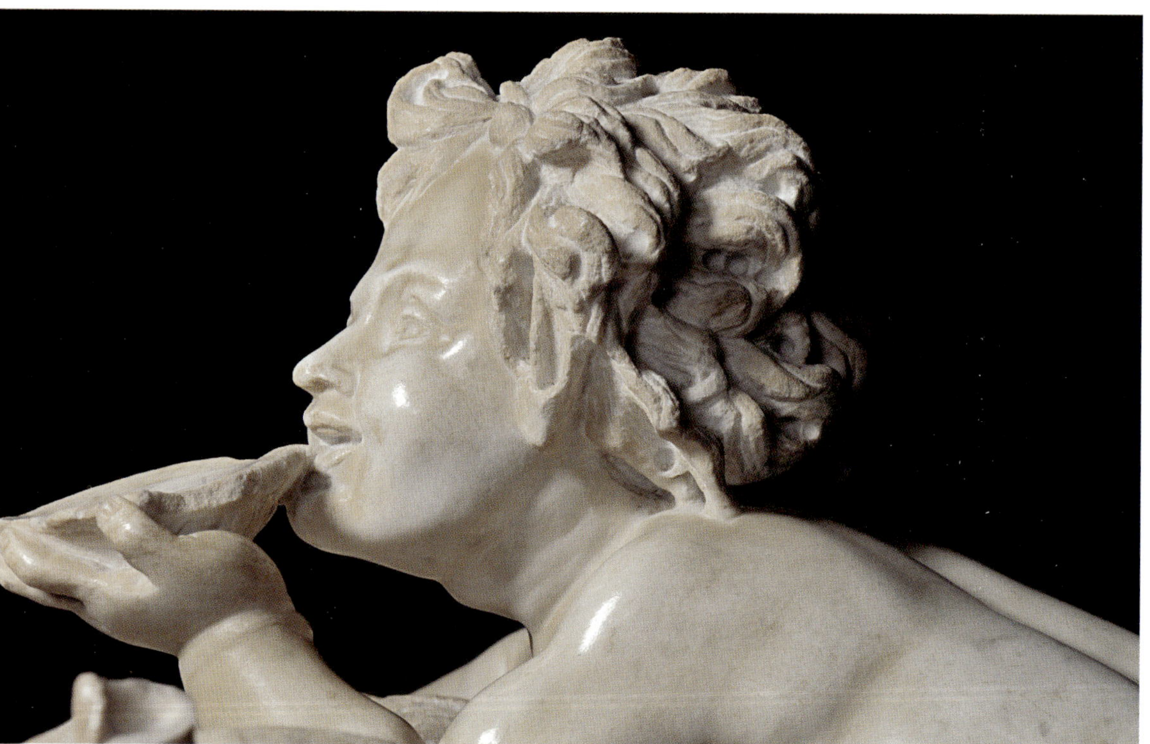

Fig. 6 (above)
G. L. Bernini, *Goat Amalthea* (before 1615), detail, Rome, Galleria Borghese.

Fig. 7 (right)
G. L. Bernini, *Portrait of Paul V* (c. 1617), Rome, Galleria Borghese.

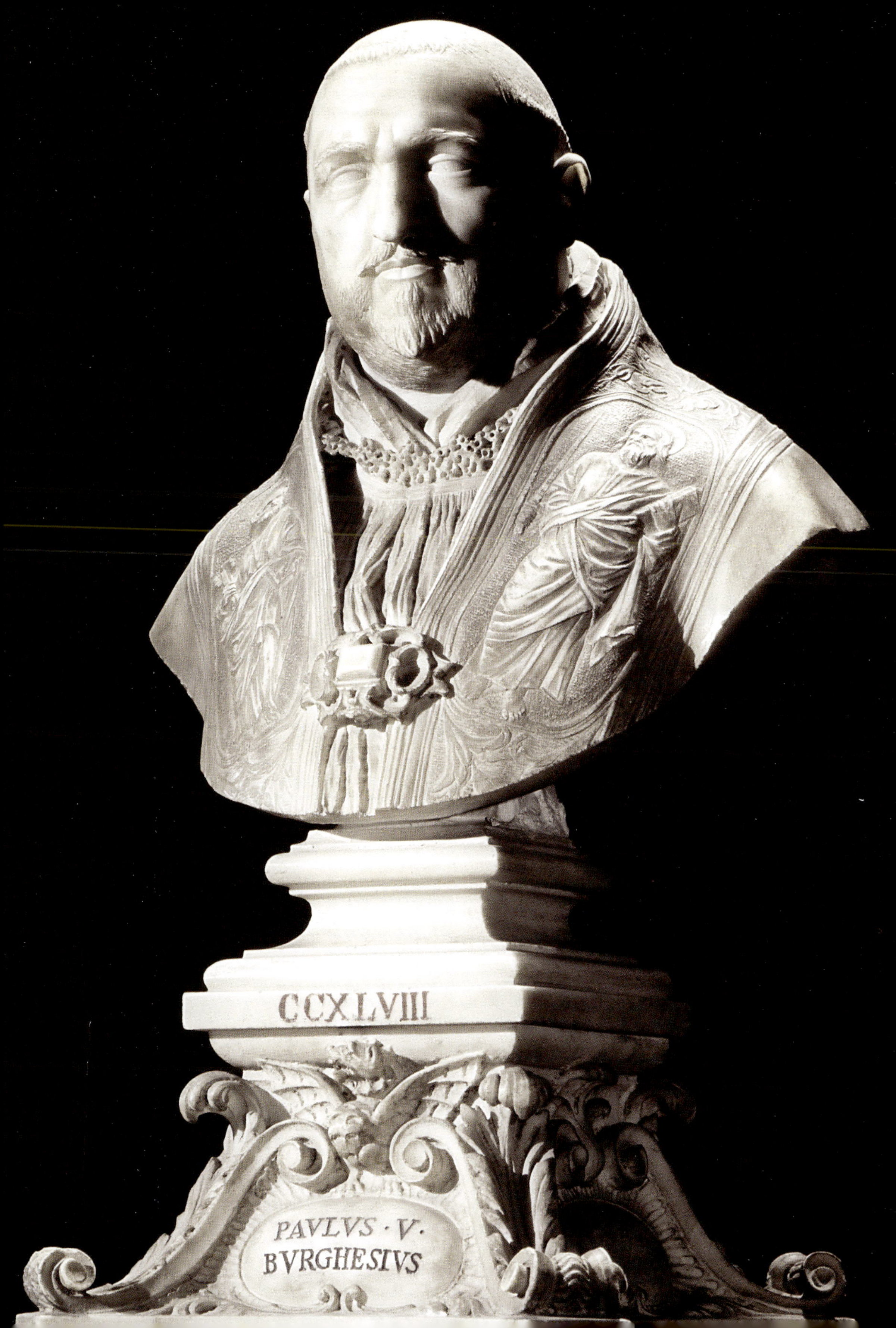
CCXLVIII
PAVLVS · V ·
BVRGHESIVS

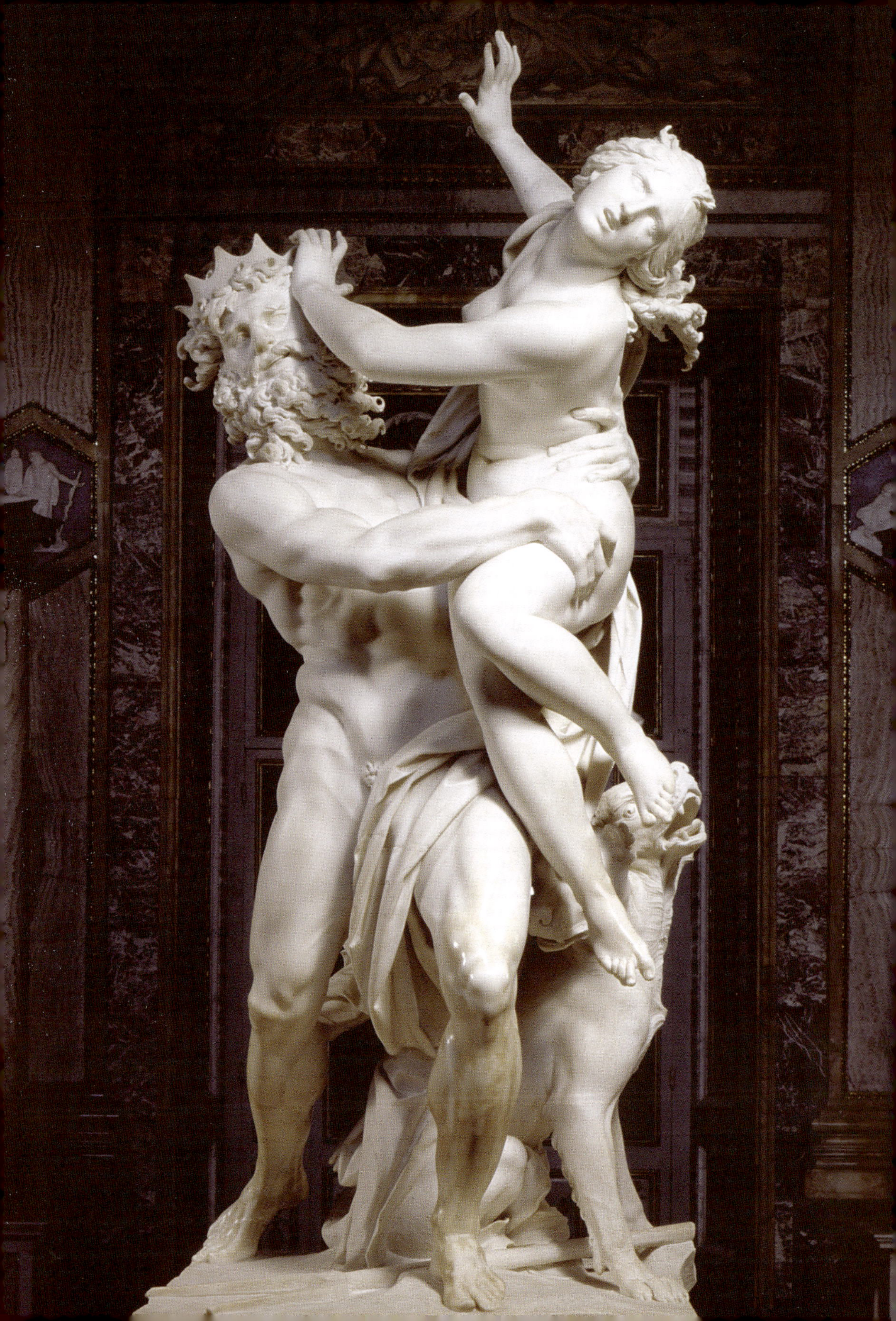

Two years later, Bernini's next work, the breathtaking *Pluto and Persephone* (Figs. 8-9) would see him continuing to develop a style already distinguished by the baroque aesthetic: although the pose is inspired by Giambologna's celebrated *Hercules and Antaeus* sculpture, Bernini's group depicting an action and narrating a story is pervaded by a totally new dynamism and intense drama: Persephone's hair and cloak, and Pluto's beard are wind-blown; the goddess is shown with her arms raised and legs bent as she desperately struggles to escape from the terrible grasp of the god who has seized her; their facial expressions – like the fearful and shocked gaze of Persephone, shown with a tear rolling sadly down her cheek – reveal a new type of emotion.

The *David* (Figs. 10-11), executed for Cardinal Peretti Montalto but later passed to Cardinal Scipione, represents yet another phase in his aesthetic search. In addition to the representation of movement, naturalistic handling and expressive emotions characterising his previous work, Bernini now introduces two new elements to his arrangement of the figure: the invasion of the observer's space and single dominant viewpoint. Bernini uses a different approach to the one used by Donatello and Michelangelo for their *Davids* by deciding to show

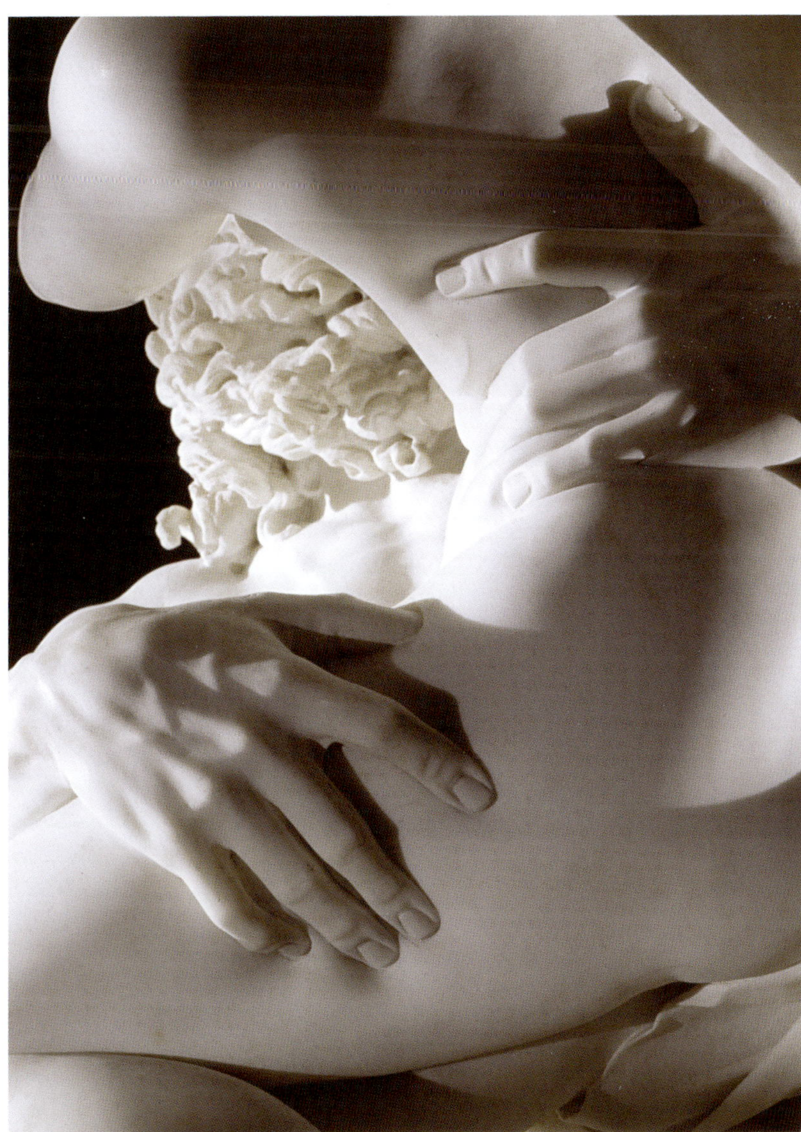

Fig. 8 (left)
G. L. Bernini,
Pluto and Persephone
(1621-22), Rome,
Galleria Borghese.

Fig. 9 (right)
G. L. Bernini,
Pluto and Persephone
(1621-22), detail, Rome,
Galleria Borghese.

his *David* in the moment of action, portraying the hero grimacing with tension and effort, his bust twisted in extreme torsion, as he prepares to release the mortal shot at an imaginary Goliath occupying the observers' space, thus involving them in this dramatic representation. In order to present the complete development of the action, the description of a theatrical drama, Bernini needed to compose his work from a single viewpoint. As observers walk around the statue they may well appreciate other details along with the exceptional technical virtuosity but they will lose the coherence of David's gesture.

We find an even more convincing version of this arrangement in Bernini's *Apollo and Daphne* (Figs. 12-14). Here too he tells a tale, the episode in which Apollo pursues Daphne who changes into a laurel tree in order to escape him, but this time he goes even further: he not only depicts the moment of action, the height of the drama, but the transitory moment of the metamorphosis. Bernini stuns us with his ability to use cold, hard, white marble to transmit the drama of the story and violence of the action

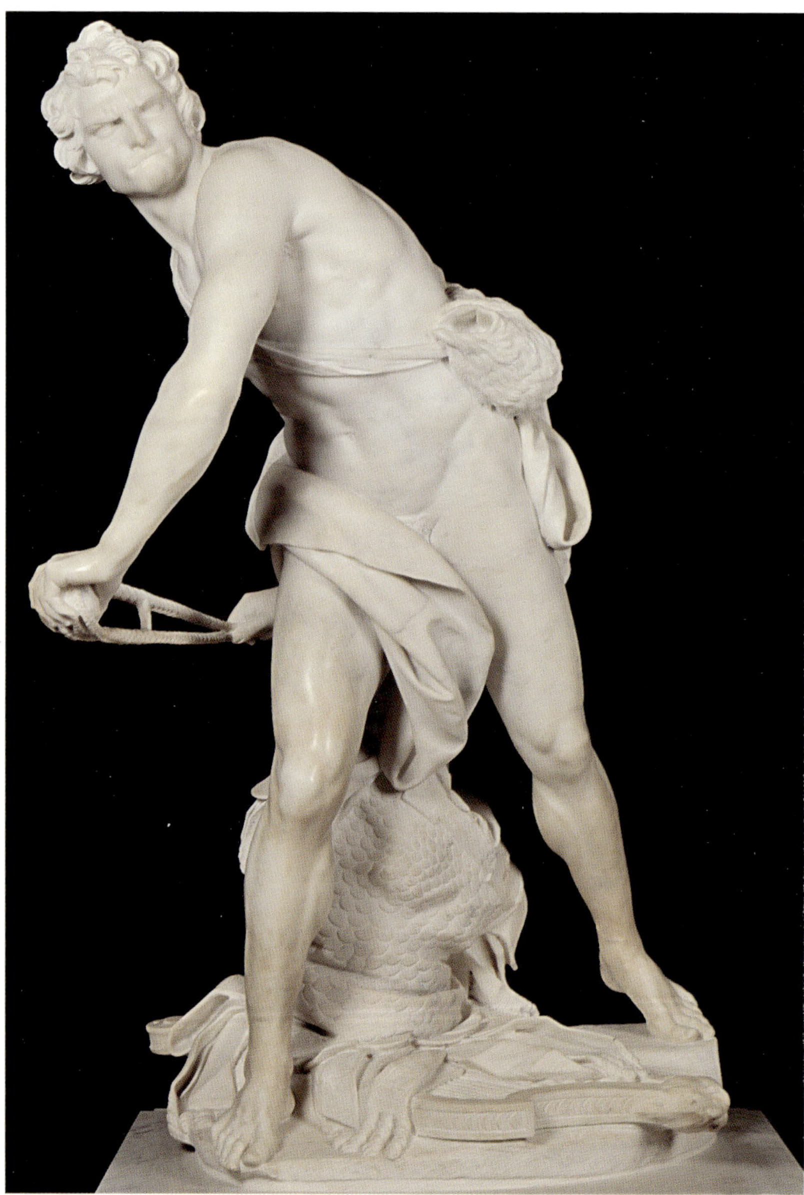

Fig. 10 (left)
G. L. Bernini, *David* (1623-24), Rome, Galleria Borghese.

Fig. 11 (right)
G. L. Bernini, *David* (1623-24), detail, Rome, Galleria Borghese.

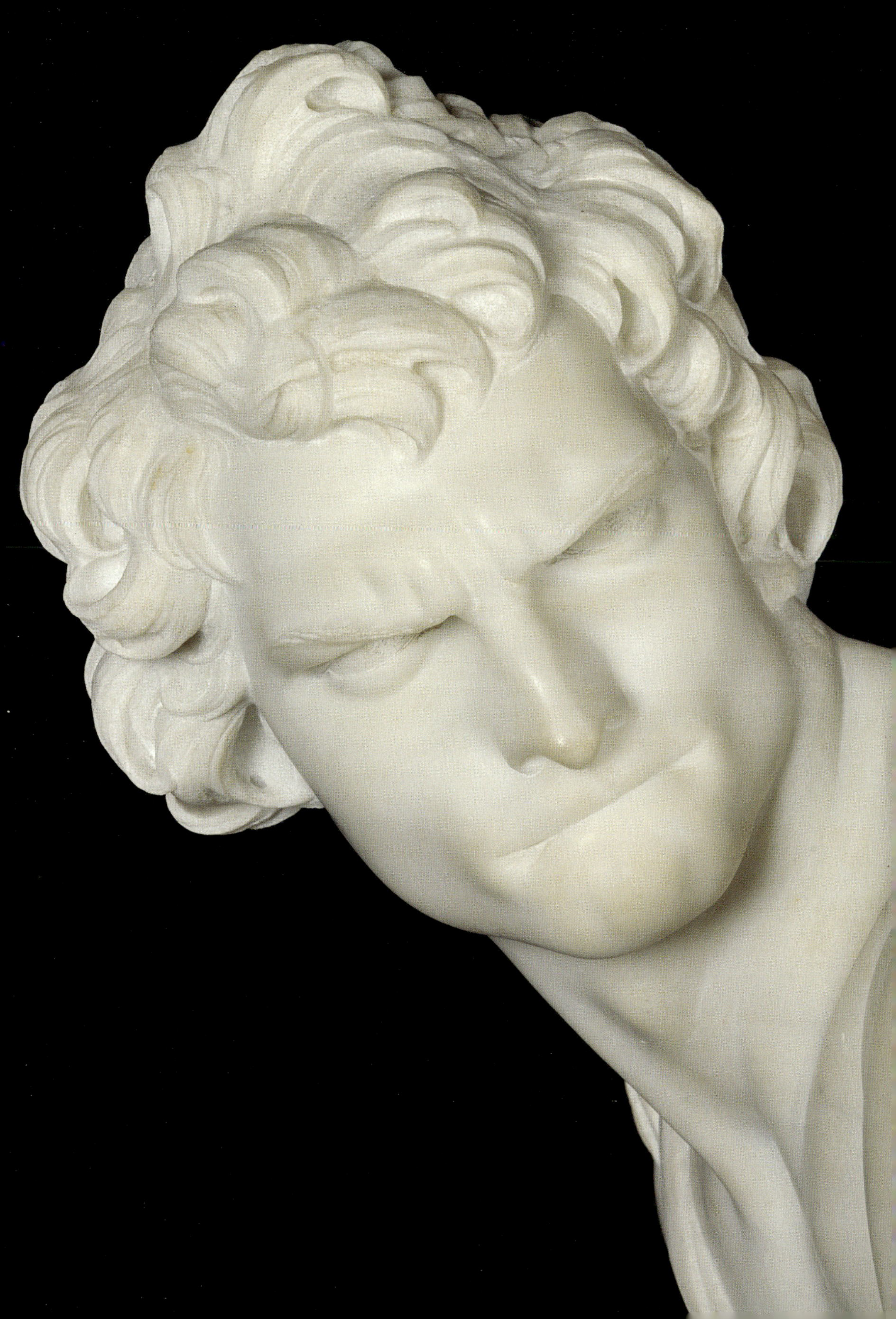

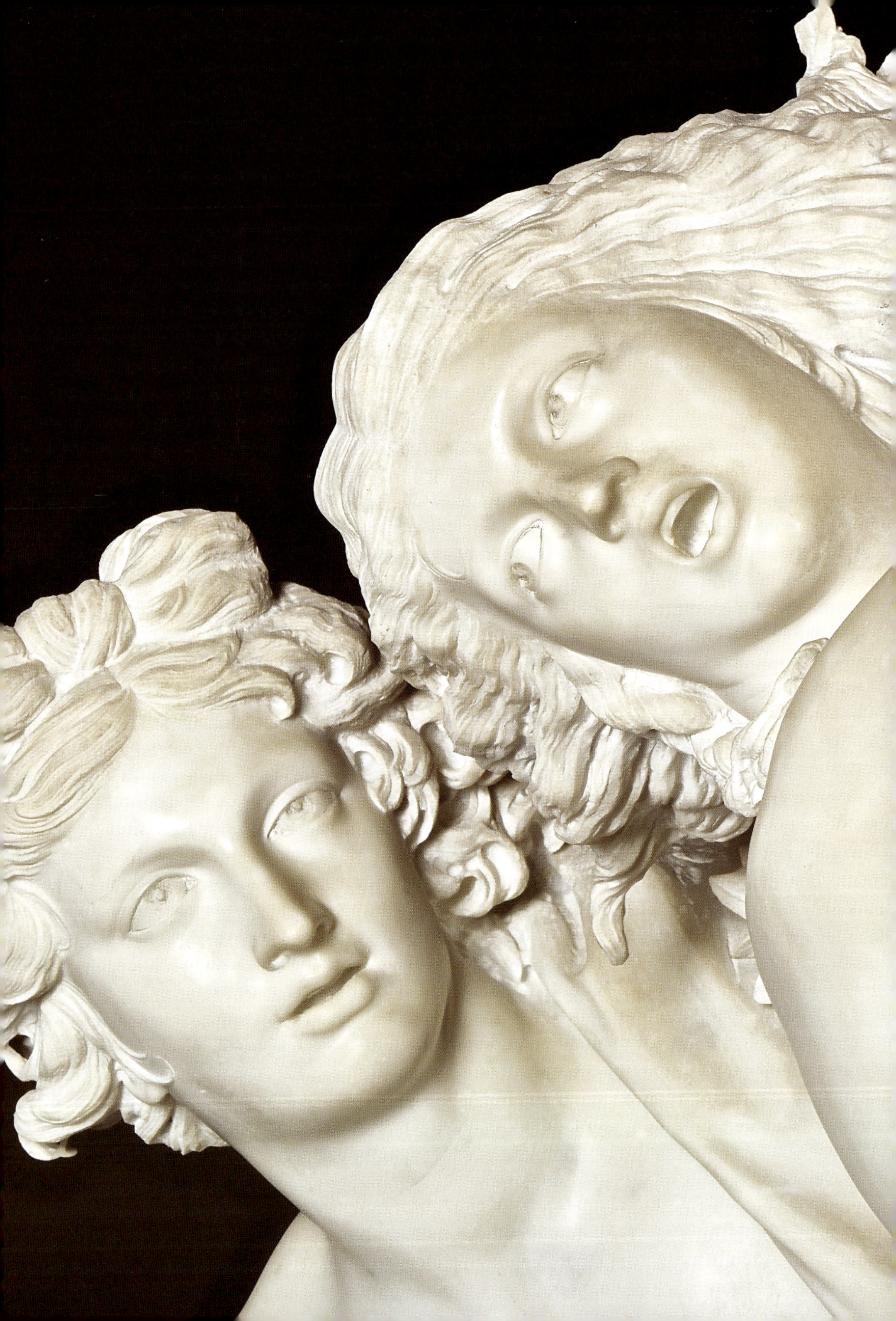

in the leap that lifts the nymph's feet from the ground, in the terrified gesture that she makes as she throws up her arms and tries to flee from the god, in her fluttering tunic, in Daphne's terrified frightened expression and in Apollo's astonished gaze. The action was so swift and dynamic that it required a single viewpoint – originally established by the artist – in order to be grasped as a whole. In fact, the *Apollo and Daphne* group was designed to stand against one of the walls of the room.

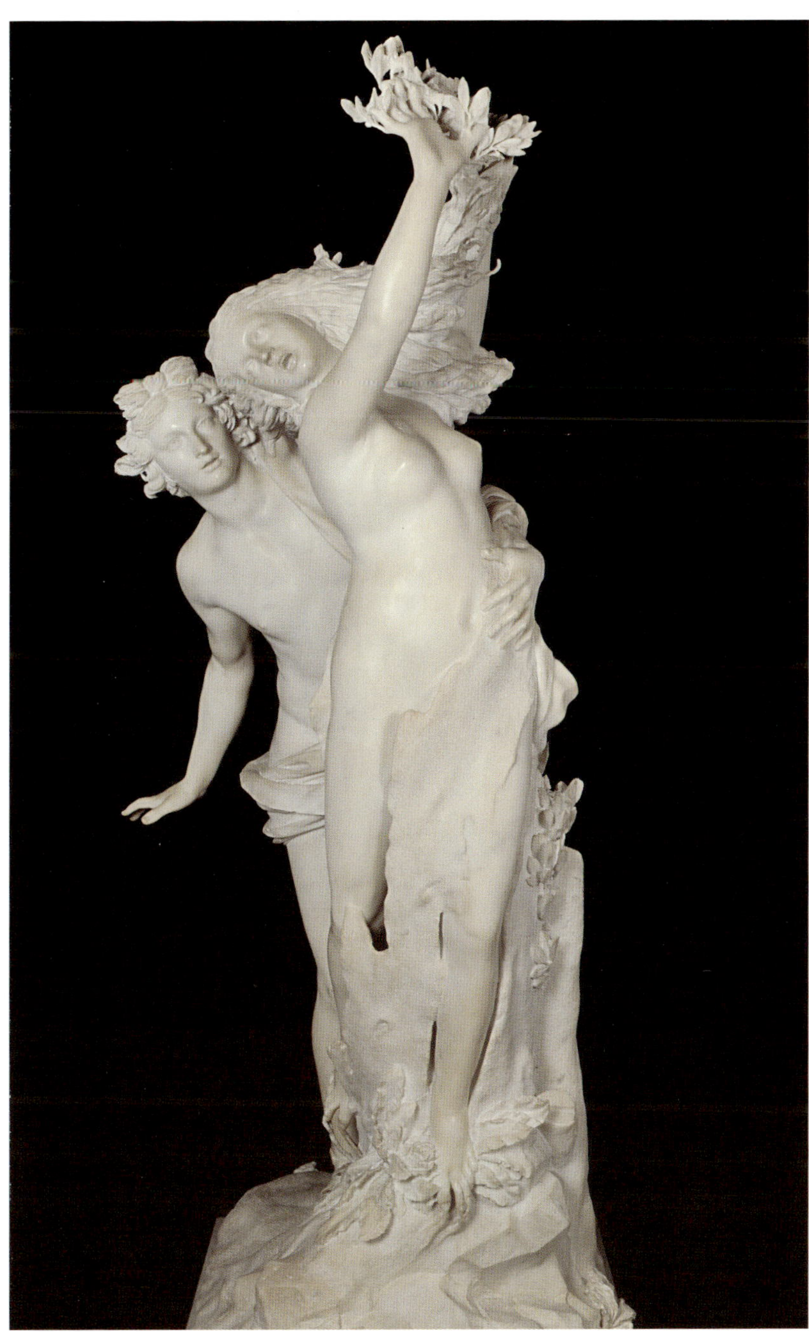

Figs. 12-13-14
(left, right and overleaf)
G. L. Bernini,
Apollo and Daphne
(1622-25),
full view and details,
Rome, Galleria Borghese.

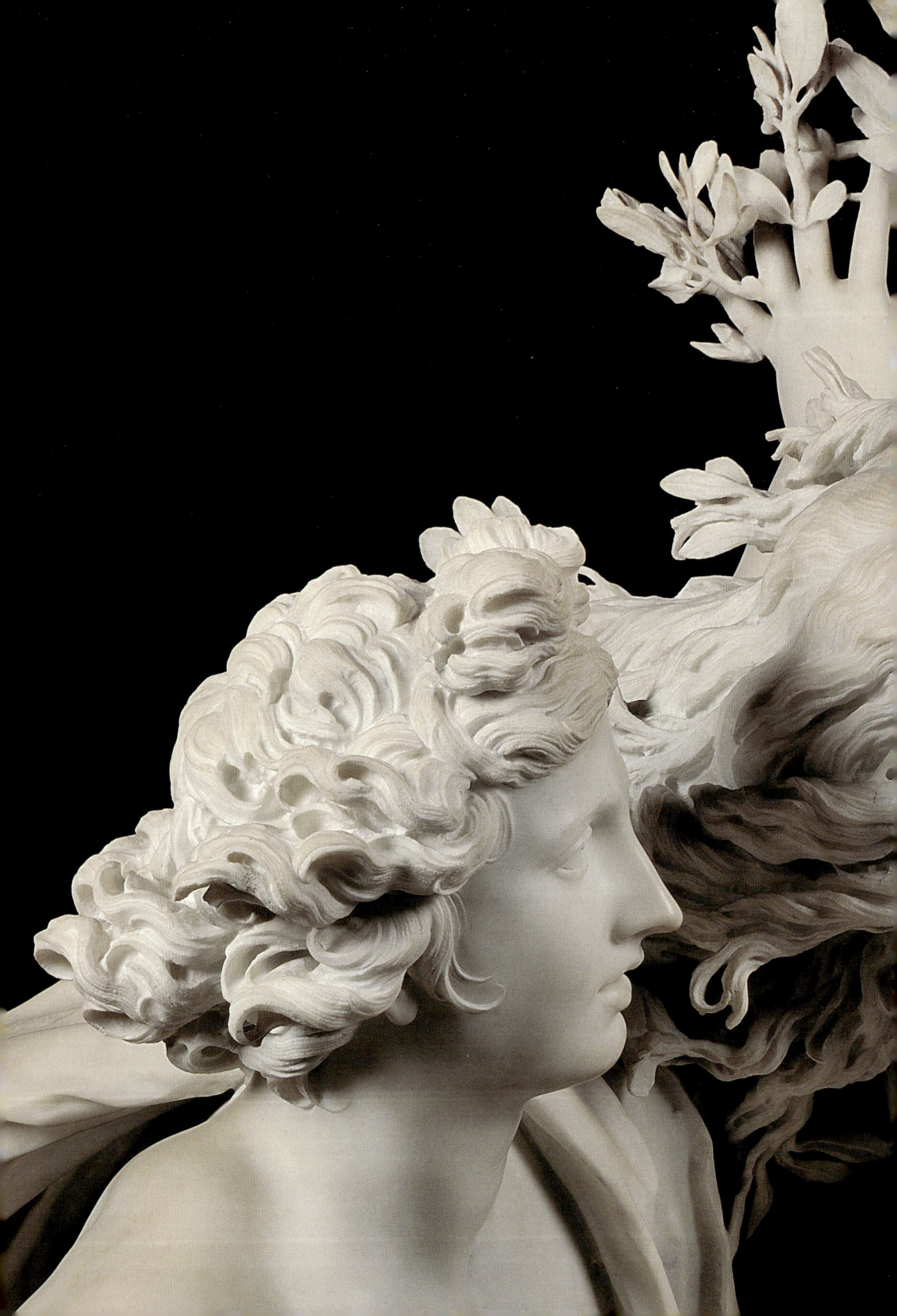

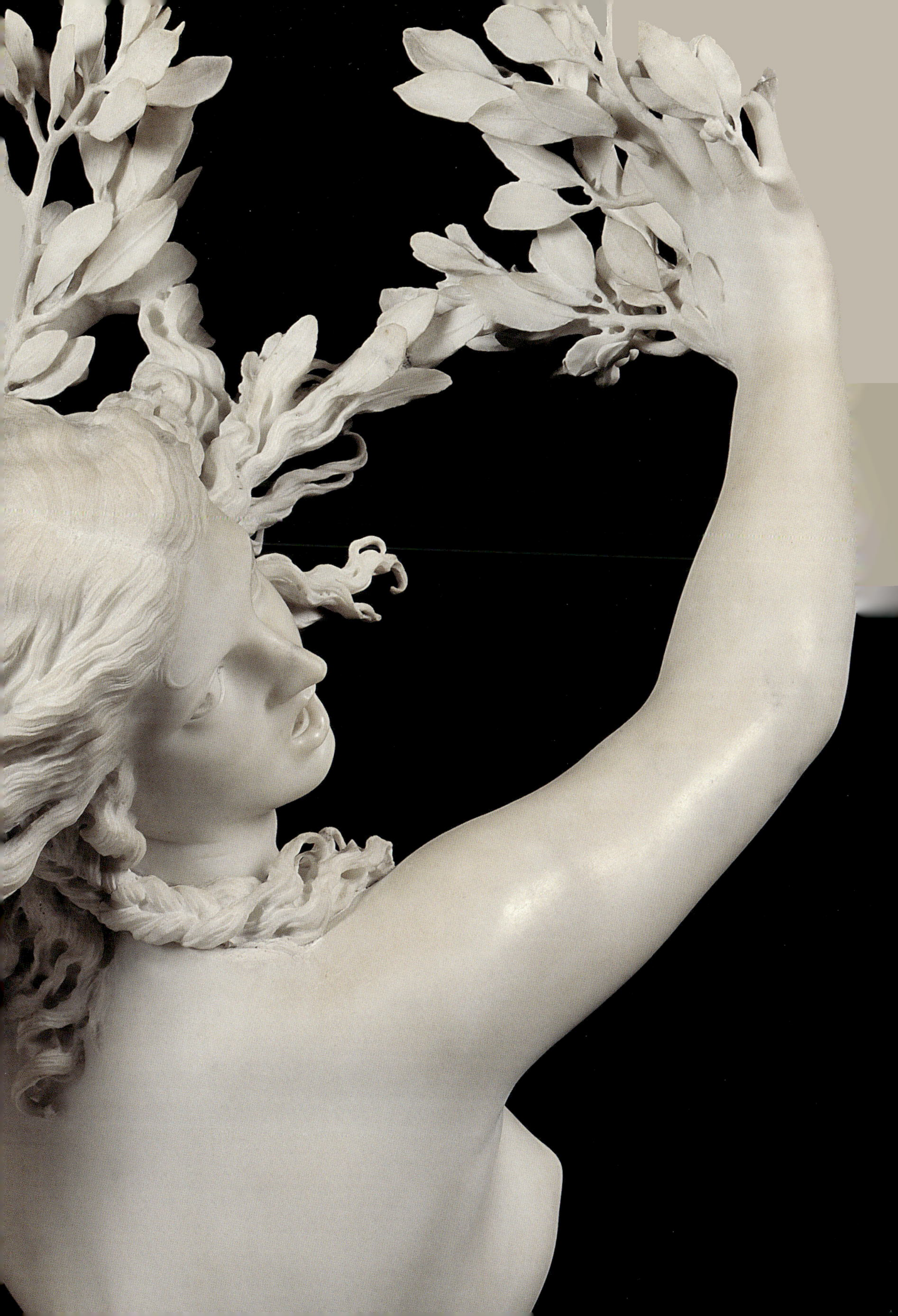

BERNINI AND URBAN VIII: THE YEARS OF MATURITY

The new spatial and emotional dimension attained by Bernini, along with the truly dazzling technical virtuosity that he displayed in his proud challenge to the perfection of classical art, many splendid examples of which were conserved in Villa Borghese, as well as to the superb art of Michelangelo, which had previously been considered insuperable, saw him emerge as victor and allowed him to acquire boundless fame in the process. After taking the papal throne in 1623, Urban VIII was keen to launch a grand campaign of artistic works and saw Bernini as the painter of genius, the modern Michelangelo, who would be capable of breathing life into his colossal projects that would not only bequeath the city of Rome a new appearance worthy of the prestigious role that the Church had reacquired but would also increase the power and prestige of his family. Bernini attained hegemony over the Roman artistic scene, exploring every field of sculpture, from statues to portraits, from funerary monuments to altars and chapels, from fountains to ephemeral decorations.

Bernini was completing the last Borghese statue group when he received a commission from Urban

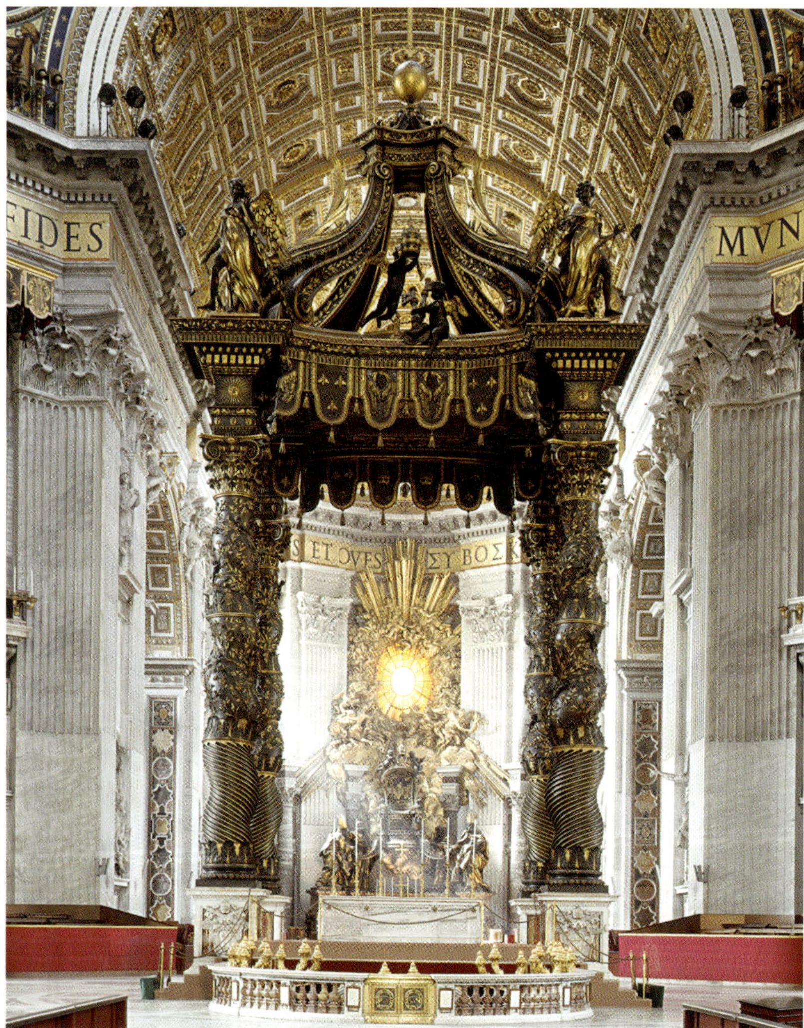

Fig. 15 (right)
G. L. Bernini,
St Bibiana (1624-26),
Rome,
Church of Santa Bibiana.

Fig. 16 (left)
G. L. Bernini,
Baldacchino
(1624-1633),
Vatican City,
St Peter's Basilica.

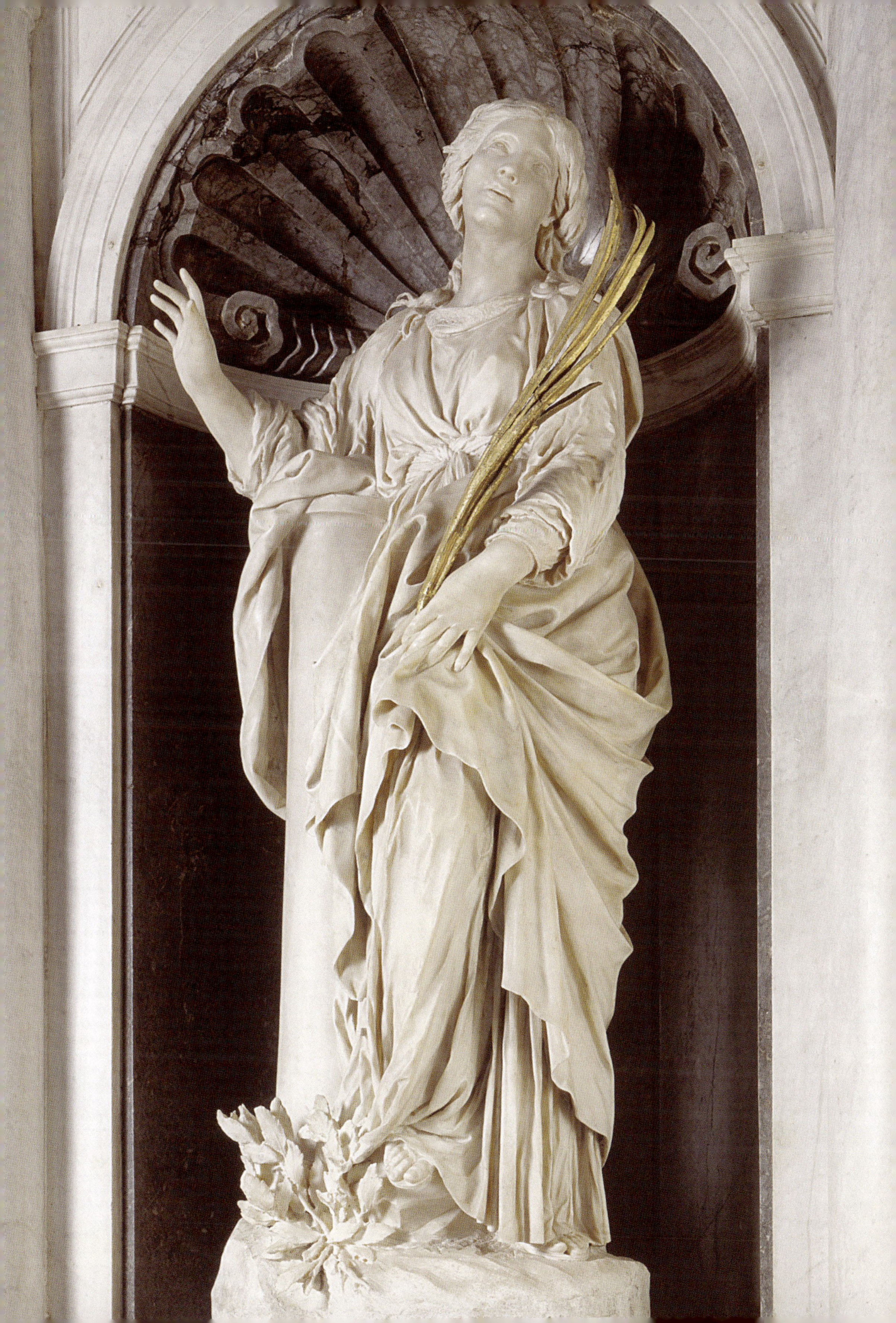

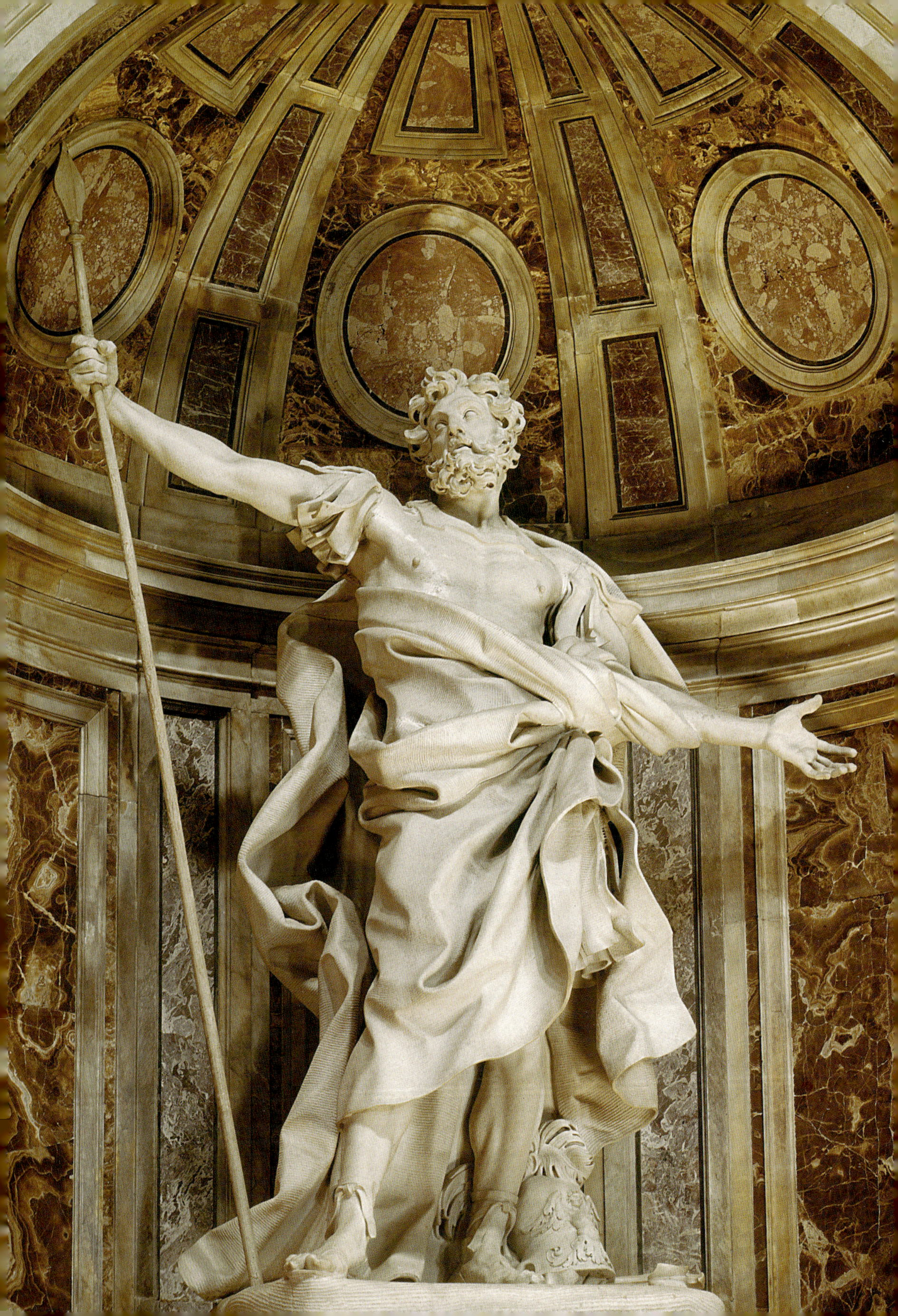

VIII to sculpt *St Bibiana* (Fig. 15) for the church of the same name, which was under restoration. Bernini depicts the saint with great naturalness and simplicity, showing her looking up towards the celestial sphere in an attitude revealing the profound devotion and divine love that led to her martyrdom, clutching the rich drapery against herself as if to underline her emotions.

For Urban VIII the most pressing task on hand was to complete the outfitting of the Vatican basilica, the temple of Christianity, a sacred site, as well as the tomb of Peter, prince of the apostles. The main focus of his attention was the crossing, the most important area in the entire basilica, both in terms of artistic importance and its religious and liturgical significance. This area was bounded by Michelangelo's immense piers and dome; it was here that the tomb of St Peter and high altar were situated, and where the most solemn and important ceremonies took place. The piers housed some of Christianity's most venerated relics. In 1624, Bernini was first commissioned by Urban VIII to create a ciborium in the traditional manner over the high altar to focus the attention of the faithful on the tomb of St Peter. The artist designed a huge spectacular structure inspired by a baldachin: by transforming the light mobile canopy usually used in processions into a mighty static monument, Bernini was able to enlarge the dimensions of the structure in proportion to the vast space of the crossing without creating a visual barrier, turning it into the perspective focus of the Basilica. The slender twisted bronze columns of the Baldacchino (Fig. 16) rise loftily upwards to support the canopy imitating a tasselled cloth, while the bronze colour stands out against the pale background of the marble revetments. The superb gilt-bronze decorations densely covering the bronze surface create luminous effects embellishing the work and endowing it with symbolic meanings, alluding in particular to the power of the pope, and thus to the power of the Church, in its almost obsessive repetition of the Barberini family's heraldic figures: bees, suns and laurel branches. In 1628, while he was still absorbed in the creation of the Baldacchino on behalf of Urban VIII, Bernini turned his attention to the actual crossing with the aim of drawing attention to the relics stored there, which included the spear of St Longinus, several fragments of the True Cross found by St Helena, the head of St Andrew and the Veil of St Veronica. Bernini divided the piers into two sections: the bottom sections had niches designed to house the four colossal statues of the saints, while the top sections contained four aedicules supported by columns from Constantine's antique *pergula* flanking a relief depicting the relic contained.

The four statues, which were made by Bernini himself (*St Longinus*), Duquesnoy (*St Andrew*), Andrea Bolgi (*St Helena*), and Francesco Mochi (*Veronica*), adopted different stylistic approaches reflecting the artistic tendencies of that period. For example, Bernini's *St Longinus* (Fig. 17), a statue with a majestic monumental aspect, ample gesture, ecstatic gaze and elaborate drapery, surpassing the others in terms of its quality, modelling and, above all, its vital charge, does not just respond to spatial and formal requirements, but also to symbolic needs; in fact, Bernini decided to portray the most intensely dramatic and emotional point of the saint's life by showing his conversion, the moment when the centurion recognised Christ's divinity and converted to the Christian faith.

Francesco Mochi had already revealed his skills and expressive abilities in the *St Martha* that he sculpted for the Barberini Chapel in Sant'Andrea della Valle; between 1629 and 1631, after a long period spent in Piacenza, he carved his *Veronica*, accentuating the dynamism of the figure by showing the saint as she steps forward decisively to present the veil with the face of Christ to the faithful, the movement underlined by her strongly swirling drapery. Although Andrea Bolgi was a keen pupil of Bernini, the majesty and controlled calm of the figure of *St Helena* reveals the influence of the classicising current represented by the painters Andrea Sacchi and Nicolas Poussin, and by the sculptors Alessandro Algardi and François Duquesnoy, and which Bernini himself had contributed to with his beautiful *Monument to Countess Matilde* in the basilica of St Peter's.

After proving himself to be a truly great sculptor with the works for Villa Borghese, Bernini expressed a new, highly original and intensely personal conception of this art through his Baldacchino and Reliquary Balconies, spectacular scenographic creations

Fig. 17 G. L. Bernini, *St Longinus* (1628-38), Vatican City, St Peter's Basilica.

masterfully drawing upon perspective, emotional content and symbolism to showcase the qualities of baroque aesthetic of which he was the sublime exponent.

The *Funerary Monument to Urban VIII* (Fig. 18), created by Bernini between 1627 and 1647, is another outstanding masterpiece revealing the artist's inventive genius, in which he completely renewed the traditional approach to tombs. Abandoning the wall tomb and drawing inspiration from Michelangelo, he designed a free-standing pyramidal tomb surmounted by the blessing pope with allegorical figures on its base, creating a model for subsequent generations. Despite the complex composition, use of different precious materials, and wealth of decorative elements, the monument stands out for its unitary yet dynamic overall impact, due, on the one hand, to the palpitating force and energy emanated by the figures, and, on the other, to the symbolic use of the materials: the white marble for the figures of *Charity* and *Justice* leaning against the base, onto which the Barberini bees alight; the sombre bronze, subtly brightened by gilt details, used for the pope, sarcophagus, and skeleton, shown as he inscribes the pope's name on a slab in an allusion to Urban's fame overcoming the limits of earthly oblivion.

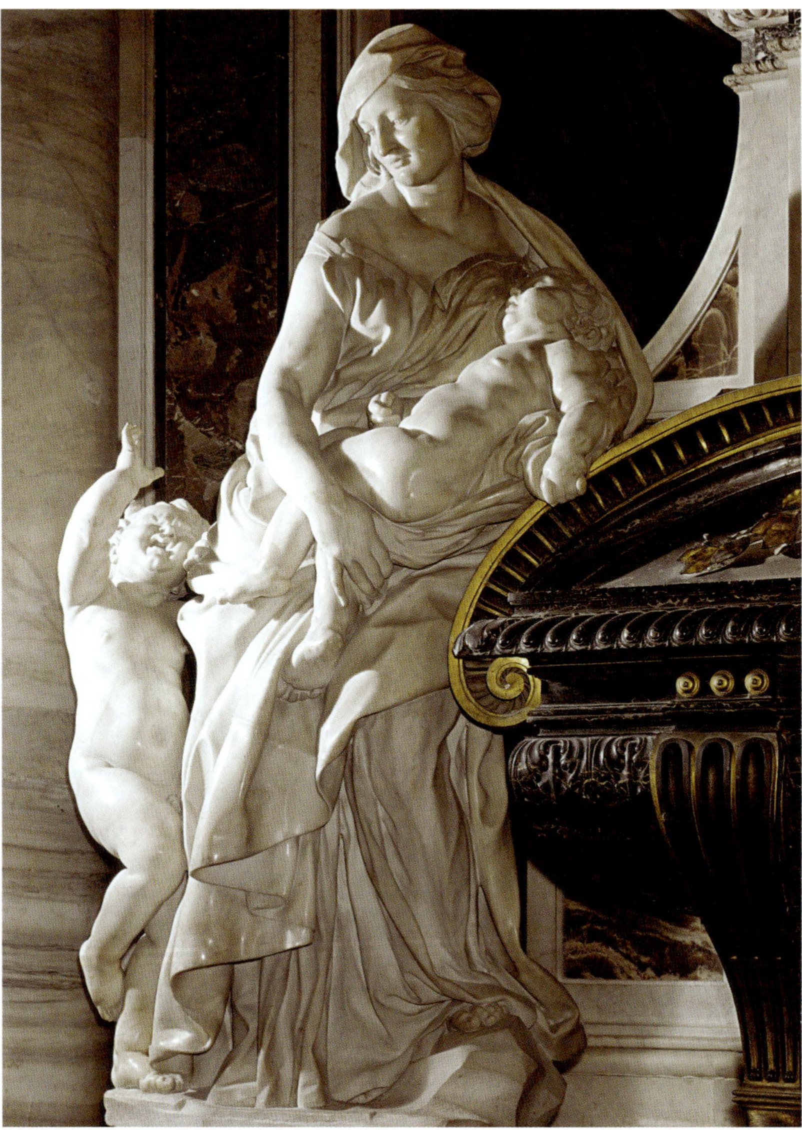

Fig. 18
G. L. Bernini,
Funerary Monument to Urban VIII (1627-47),
detail of *Charity*,
Vatican City,
St Peter's Basilica.

THE PORTRAIT GALLERY

When Orfeo Boselli claimed that "all sculptures are basically portraits" in his *Osservazioni sulla scultura antica*, the famous treatise written between 1642 and 1662, he really meant that the portrait was the genre of sculpture most requested and sought-after by patrons, both as portraits intended for funerary monuments as well as busts for their palaces. Bernini also excelled in this field, surpassing his contemporaries in his ability to capture the likeness and vitality of the personage, qualities that were particularly appreciated in portraits.

According to his biographers – and confirmed by recent studies – the first works executed by the young Bernini were the portraits of *Giovan Battista Santoni* (1610-15) in Santa Prassede and the *Bust of Antonio Coppola* (1612) in San Giovanni dei Fiorentini, which were probably entrusted to him by his father Pietro, who had never ventured into this field of sculpture before. Bernini's incredible talent emerged in the extraordinary vitality and psychological depth of these two portraits, in their natural expressions. An anecdote relates that upon seeing the *Portrait of Monsignor Pedro Foix de Montoya* (Fig. 19) on his tomb in Santa Maria di Monserrato executed in 1622, Cardinal Maffeo Barberini was so impressed by the likeness that he exclaimed: "It seems to me that Monsignor Montoya resembles his portrait!"

The diary written during Bernini's travels in France by the French collector and writer, Paul Fréart de Chantelou, recorded Bernini's observations on the difficulties involved in executing a marble portrait: he remarks that "if someone dyed their hair, beard, eyebrows, and possibly even their pupils and lips, and appeared in this state, even someone used to seeing them every day would find it difficult to recognise them". This is why it is so difficult to create a

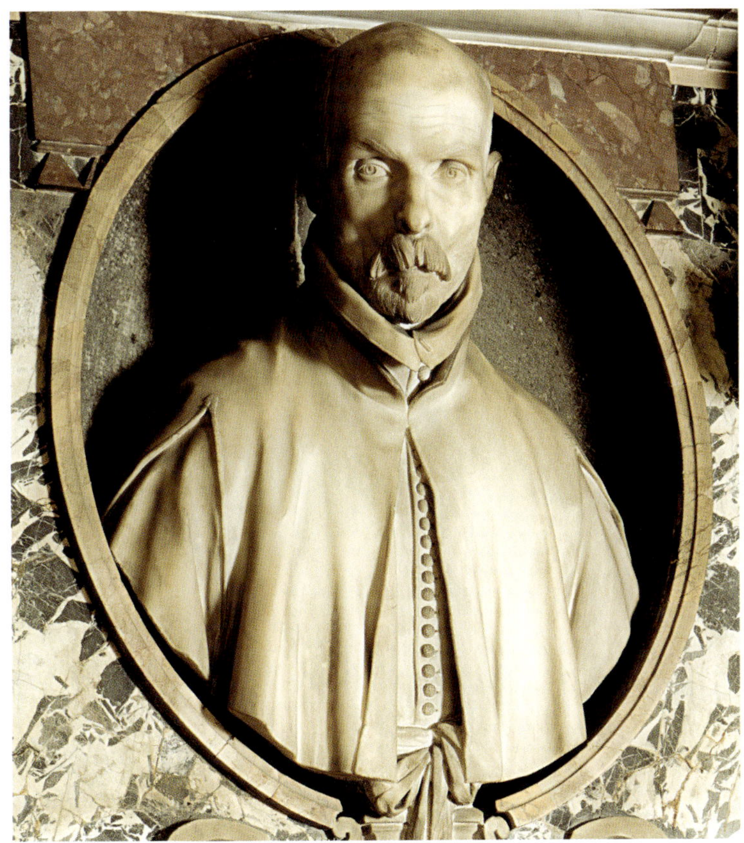

Fig. 19
G. L. Bernini,
Portrait of Monsignor Pedro Foix de Montoya (1622), Rome, Church of Santa Maria di Monserrato.

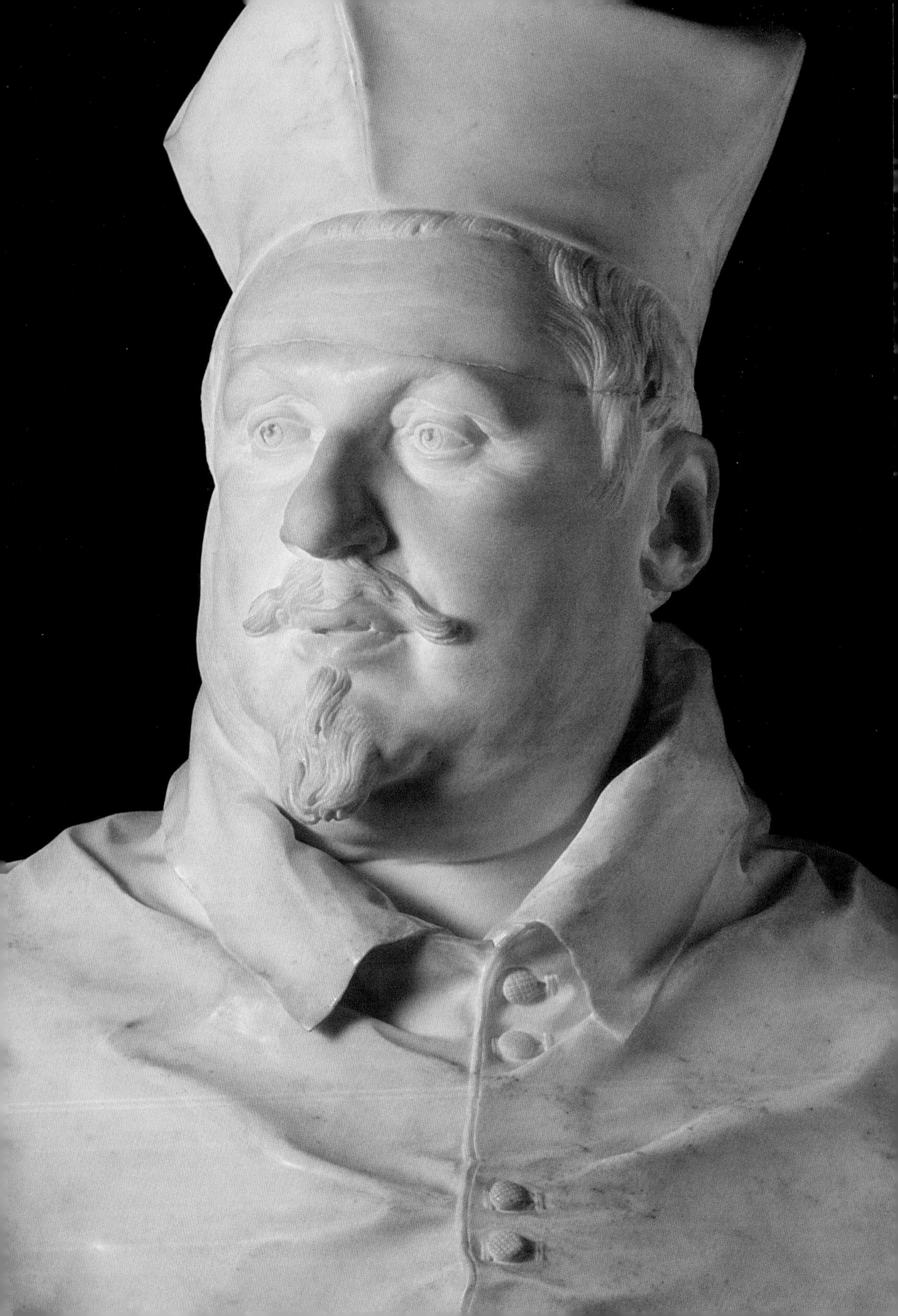

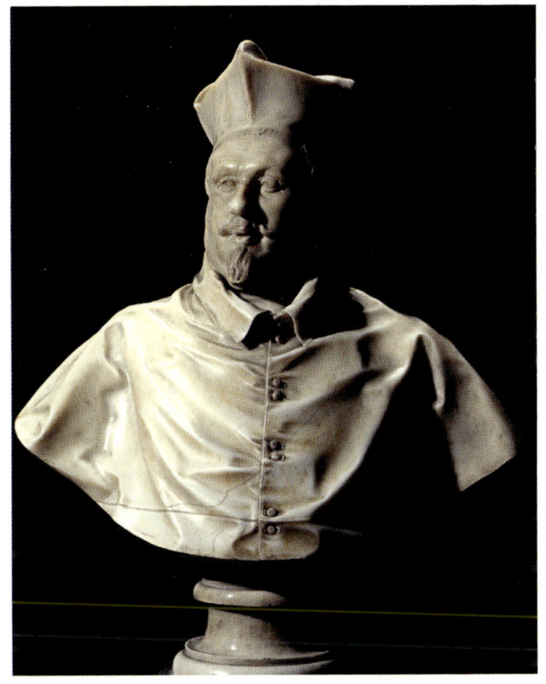

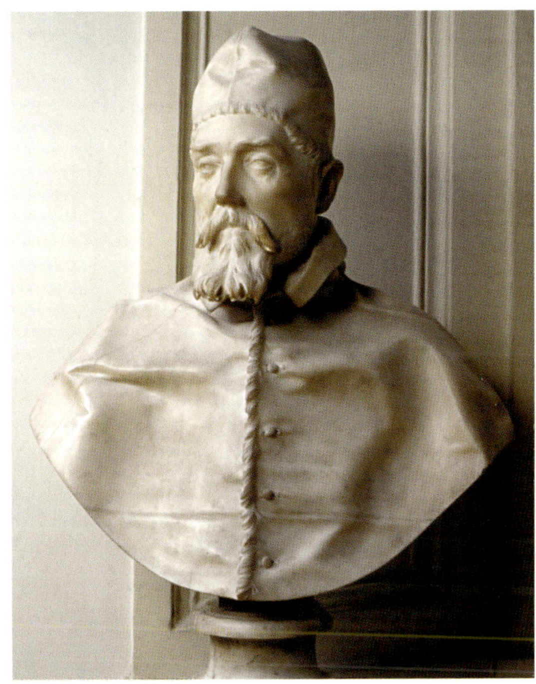

marble portrait that is a true likeness, sometimes making it necessary to force nature using optical tricks to maintain the effect of the proportions. He went on to tell Chantelou how he made his portraits; he did not like his subjects to sit still in front of him but preferred them to move and talk because it was only by portraying their natural movements and expressions that he could capture the spirit and character of the personage. In addition to his outstanding ability to portray human spirit, Bernini also possessed superb technical skills, which allowed him to model marble like wax, and thus render the softness of the skin, the depth of the wrinkles, the expression in his subjects' eyes, and even their beard bristles and the movement of their lips.

Bernini's fame as a portrait artist soon spread through the European courts, and the illustrious personages of the time, along with popes and Roman cardinals, all vied to be portrayed by him. The gallery of portraits executed by Bernini is breathtaking: *Paul V* and *Cardinal Scipione Borghese* (Figs. 20-21; Rome, Galleria Borghese), the *Bust of Cardinal Roberto Bellarmino* (Rome, Church of the Gesù), *Portrait of Gregory XV* (Toronto, the Art Gallery of Ontario), numerous portraits of Urban VIII (Fig. 22) and of other members of the Barberini family, the *Portrait of Costanza Bonarelli* (Florence, Museo del Bargello), as well as his portraits of *Monsignor Carlo Antonio dal Pozzo* (Edinburgh, the National Gallery), *Thomas Baker* (London, Victoria and Albert Museum), *Cardinal Richelieu* (Fig. 23; Paris, Musée du Louvre), *Innocent X* (Rome, Galleria Doria Pamphilj), *Francesco I d'Este* (Fig. 24; Modena, Galleria Estense) and *Louis XIV* (Paris, Musée du Louvre), along with the terracotta *Alexander VII* (Rome, Galleria Nazionale d'Arte Antica in Palazzo Corsini), to mention only the most famous pieces.

His *Bust of Scipione Borghese* (Fig. 21) executed in 1632 is one of his most famed works and was made in two versions. When Bernini was on the verge of completing the first version (Fig. 20) he discovered a flaw running across the cardinal's forehead that transformed the features of his face. Not in the least discouraged, Bernini bought another block of marble and carved the second version in just fifteen days so as not to disappoint the cardinal who could not

Figs. 20-21 (left and top left)
G. L. Bernini, *Portrait of Cardinal Borghese* (1632), Rome, Galleria Borghese.

Fig. 22 (top right)
G. L. Bernini, *Portrait of Urban VIII* (1637-38), Rome, Galleria Nazionale d'Arte Antica di Palazzo Barberini.

wait to see the finished work. The *Bust of Scipione Borghese* exemplifies the characteristics of Bernini's busts: rather than depicting the subject in a static pose, it immortalises him as he is turning his head to one side, his attention drawn by something, his lips parted in surprise; his piercing gaze, masterful bearing and physical presence make him appear alive and breathing, and transmit his despotic and determined nature.

The unbridled sensuality of Bernini's *Portrait of Costanza Bonarelli* epitomises his ability to capture the intimate expression of his sitters. Executed in 1636-38, just a few years after Cardinal Scipione's portrait, the bust depicts the wife of one of Bernini's collaborators, Matteo Bonarelli, for whom he had lost his head. Costanza was later at the centre of a scandal, which came about when Bernini discovered that she was also the mistress of his brother, Luigi Bernini. Overcome by rage Gian Lorenzo savagely beat his brother and sent a servant to slash his mistress' face.

An equally celebrated and seminal portrait was his bust of *Francesco I d'Este* (Fig. 24), supreme expression of the Baroque language and of the scenographic and dramatic taste of the period. In this work (and in his later *Portrait of Louis XIV)* Bernini focuses less on naturalism and on capturing the likeness and vital presence of his subject than on the magnificent expression of power and his subject's majestic and regal appearance. The austere imperious face, flowing locks and rich swirling drapery all contribute to an ideal portrait exalting the role of prince and affirming the importance of the Este house, an aim particularly close to the heart of Francesco I.

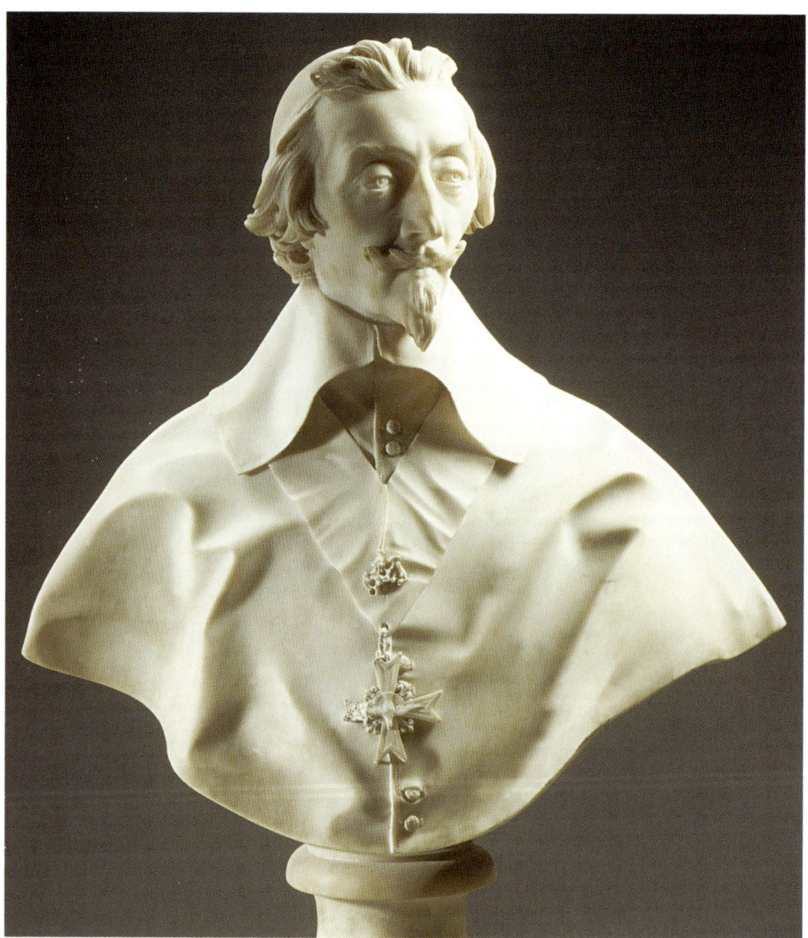

Fig. 23 (left)
G. L. Bernini, *Portrait of Cardinal Richelieu* (1640-41), Paris, Musée du Louvre.

Fig. 24 (right)
G. L. Bernini, *Portrait of Francesco I d'Este* (1650-51), Modena, Galleria Estense.

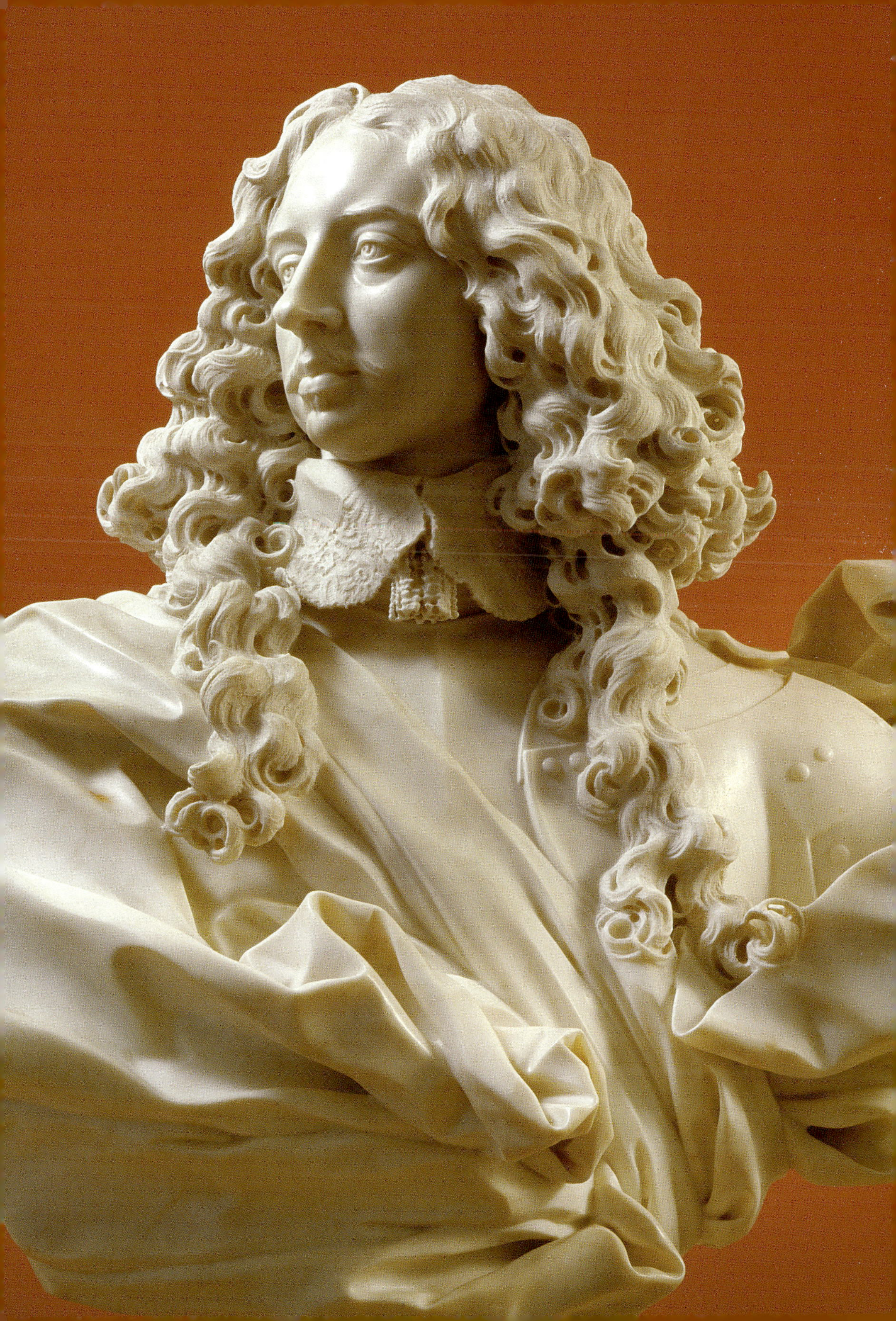

THE FOUNTAINS

Bernini's creative flair combined with his innate love of drama led him to create some of the most unusual and striking fountains to embellish Rome. Fountains are an important feature of Rome's urban landscape, and from the 16th century onwards – and during the papacy of Gregory XIII in particular – fountains multiplied in numerous sites throughout the city. Bernini turned these fountains into major landmarks transforming the sites where they stood and symbolising them, exalting the role of water in a unitary composition blending natural with architectural and sculptural elements, releasing an intense vitality that saw bees, dolphins, tritons, seashells and animals combined with water features, and assuming vast allegorical meanings alluding to his patrons and historical events. In 1623-24, Bernini's father Pietro was made commissioner and inspector of the conduits for Piazza Navona's fountains and architect of the Acqua Vergine aqueduct system, and in 1624 Gian Lorenzo was appointed superintendent of the Acqua Felice acqueduct by Urban VIII; it may have been then that Gian Lorenzo developed his special relationship with water, an element that he loved, confiding in Chantelou: "I am a friend of water; it does my temperament good". In his *Fountain of the Barcaccia* (Fig. 25) in Piazza di Spagna, executed between 1627-29,

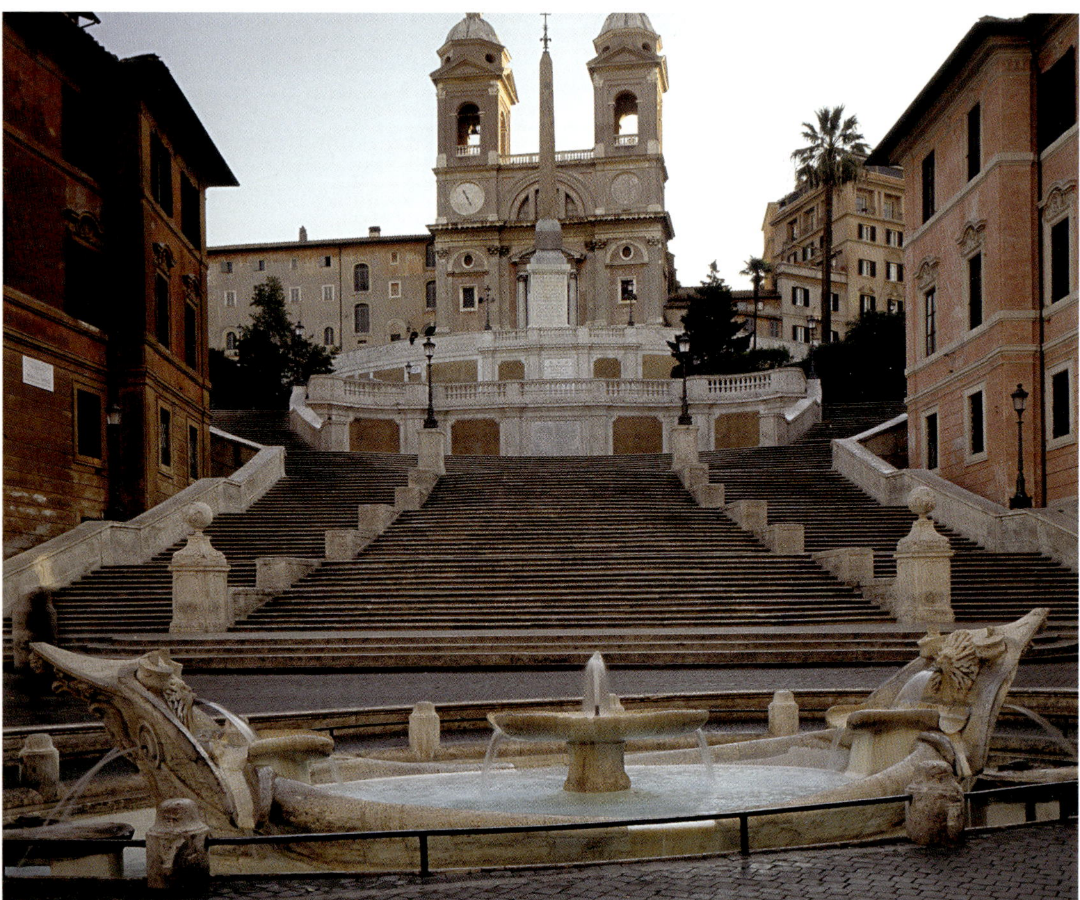

Fig. 25 (above) Pietro and G. L. Bernini, *Fountain of the Barcaccia* (1627-29), Rome, Piazza di Spagna.

Fig. 26 (right) G. L. Bernini, *Fountain of the Triton* (1642-43), Rome, Piazza Barberini.

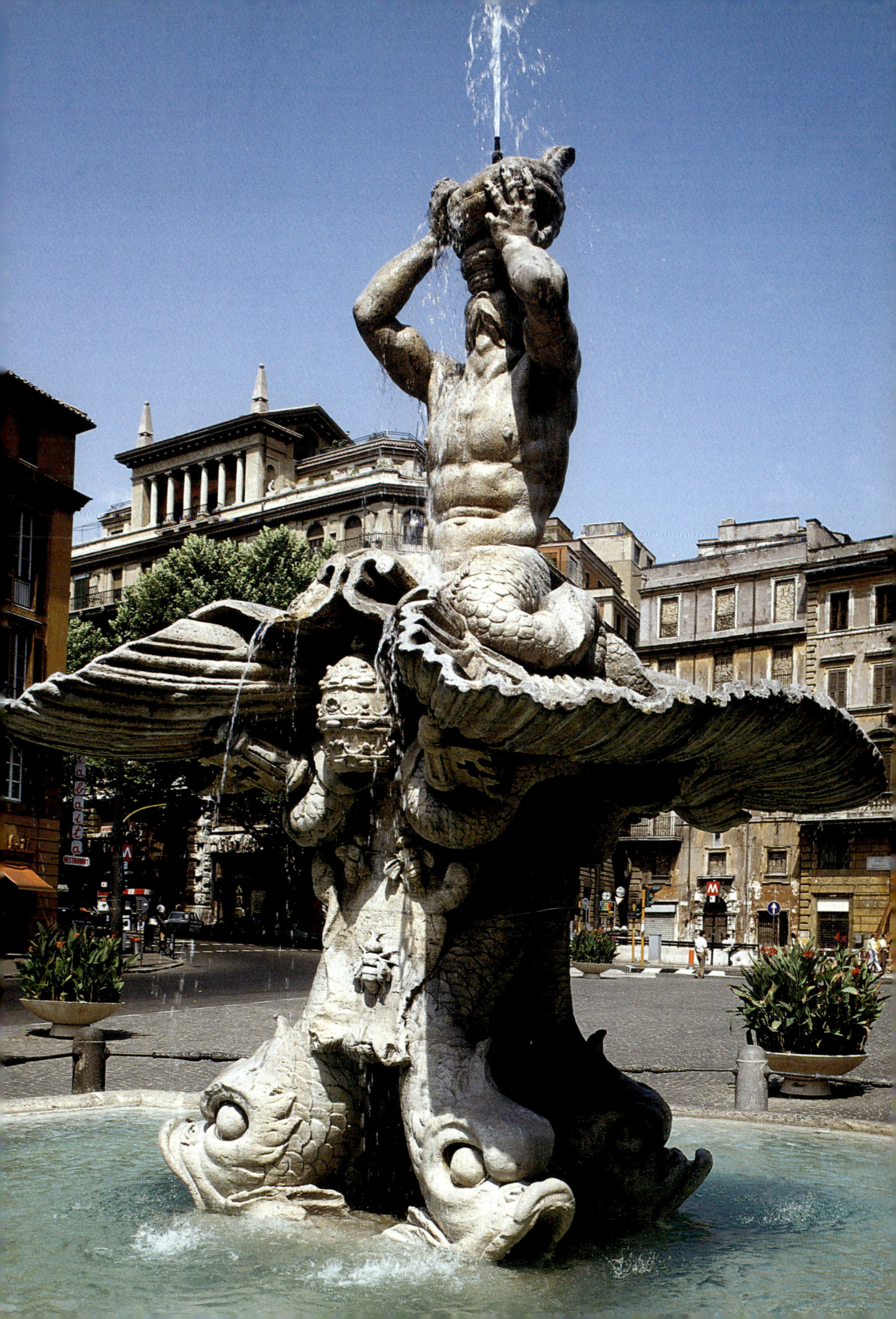
RESTAURANT
M

the artist overcomes the technical difficulties resulting from the low water pressure, which would have prevented him from creating water effects and jets, by creating an unusual composition that transforms the fountain into a water-filled boat on the verge of sinking. The suns and coats of arms embellishing the craft are intended to remind the Romans that it was thanks to the pope's munificence that they were being supplied with water.

When he created his *Fountain of the Triton* (Fig. 26) in Piazza Barberini Bernini produced yet another superb masterpiece. Pope Urban VIII commissioned this work from the artist with the intention of conferring a powerful image upon the piazza forming the courtyard of his magnificent new family palace, and Gian Lorenzo responded by designing a group of dolphins entwining their tails to support the papal tiara and keys, their bodies bearing the papal insignia. A mighty triton kneels in the huge shell supported by the dolphins and blows into a conch from which water gushes in a jet that would originally have been far more powerful and noisy. The jet represents the sound of a trumpet calling attention to the residence of the powerful papal family.

Nearby, on the corner of the Via Veneto stands the *Fountain of Bees*, another small masterpiece sculpted by Bernini during the same period, consisting of a bi-valve shell featuring the Barberini bees that stands open to collect the water.

A few years later, in 1648-51, Bernini designed his *Fountain of the Four Rivers* (Fig. 27-28) for Piazza Navona. Here, as in Piazza di Spagna and Piazza Barberini, Bernini's fountain would become the emblematic feature of its site. The project, commissioned by Pope Innocent X, was originally assigned to Francesco Borromini, who had proposed a highly symbolic yet straightforward design. Thanks to the intervention of the pope's sister-in-law, Donna Olimpia Maidalchini, Bernini succeeded in getting a silver model of his fountain to the pope. Innocent X was so struck by the fantasy and opulence of this fountain that he entrusted the project to Bernini. The underlying concept of the composition is the Church's power and hegemony over the entire world, expressed through the figure of the pope. Reclining on a central rocky formation and flanked by plants and animals were the allegorical figures of the four rivers alluding to the four continents: the Ganges (Asia), the Nile (Africa), the Danube (Europe) and the Rio della Plata (America); looming over the fountain is an obelisk on top of which the Pamphilj dove is perched, the heraldic symbol of Pope Innocent X, which identifies this as a monument to the power of the pope and the Church. It also affirms the supremacy of the Catholic religion and the triumph of the Church, which, thanks to the Society of Jesus and its missionary initiatives, had spread throughout the world. In artistic terms, the fountain forms a vital plastic complex full of life and movement: the allegorical figures gesticulate in various positions, the palm bends in the wind, the lion is leaning down towards the water basin with his mighty body (Fig. 27), the horse emerges from the cavity opposite while the water gushes into the basin where dolphins swim. The rocky outcrop in the centre contradicts the constructional logic that would have demanded a more compact area in the point where the high obelisk stands. In his biography of his father, Domenico Bernini dwells on this particular aspect which caused Innocent X to marvel that "the huge bulk of the obelisk with its great pedestal could be supported by a rock hollowed out on all sides". He also narrates how the pope went to see the fountain before it was completed. Exceedingly impressed, Innocent asked Bernini when he would be able to see the water running through it but was told by Bernini that more time was required. As the pope was walking off, Bernini gave a secret signal to turn the water on and Innocent turned to see "a spectacle that caused him to remain ecstatic with wonder".

In this undertaking, the master was helped by his assistants, Giacomo Antonio Fancelli, Claudio Poussin, Antonio Raggi, and Francesco Baratta, who executed the figures of the rivers, while he personally carved the rocky outcrop.

Fig. 27 (right) G. L. Bernini, *Fountain of the Four Rivers*, (1648-51), detail of lion, Rome, Piazza Navona.

Fig. 28 (overleaf) G. L. Bernini, *Fountain of the Four Rivers*, (1648-51), Rome, Piazza Navona.

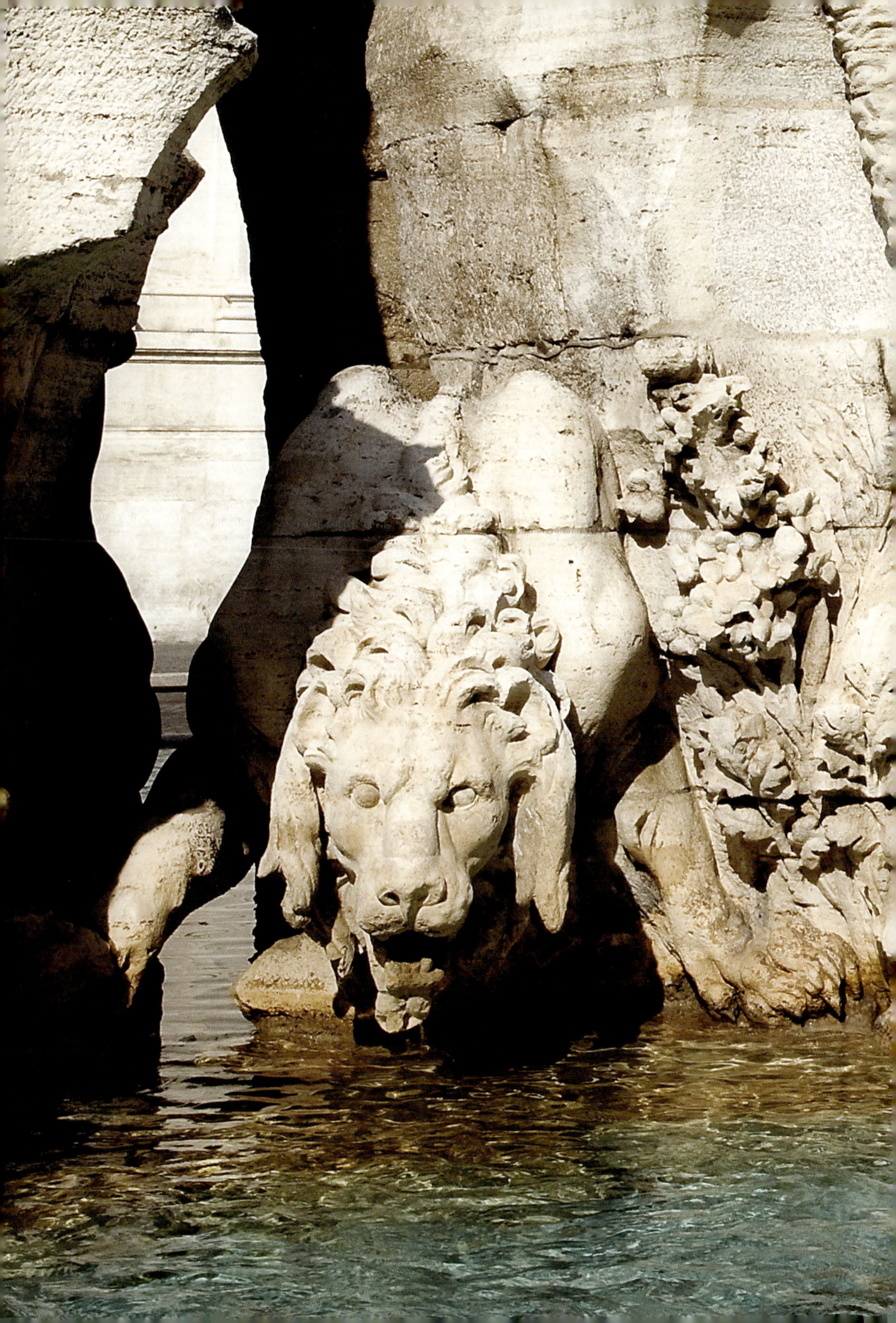

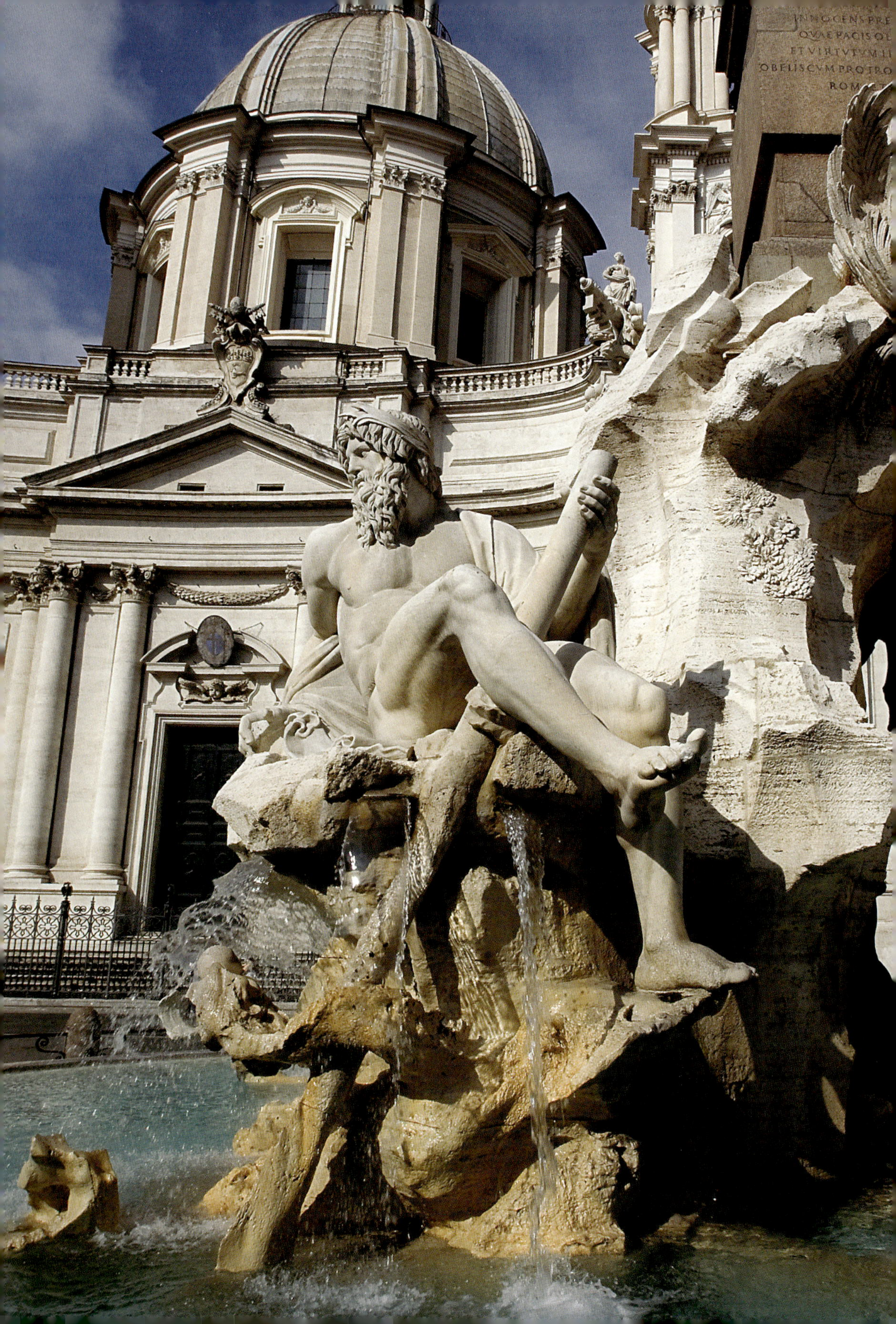
INNOCENS PRE
QVAE PACIS O
ET VIRTVTVM
OBELISCVM PROTRO
ROM

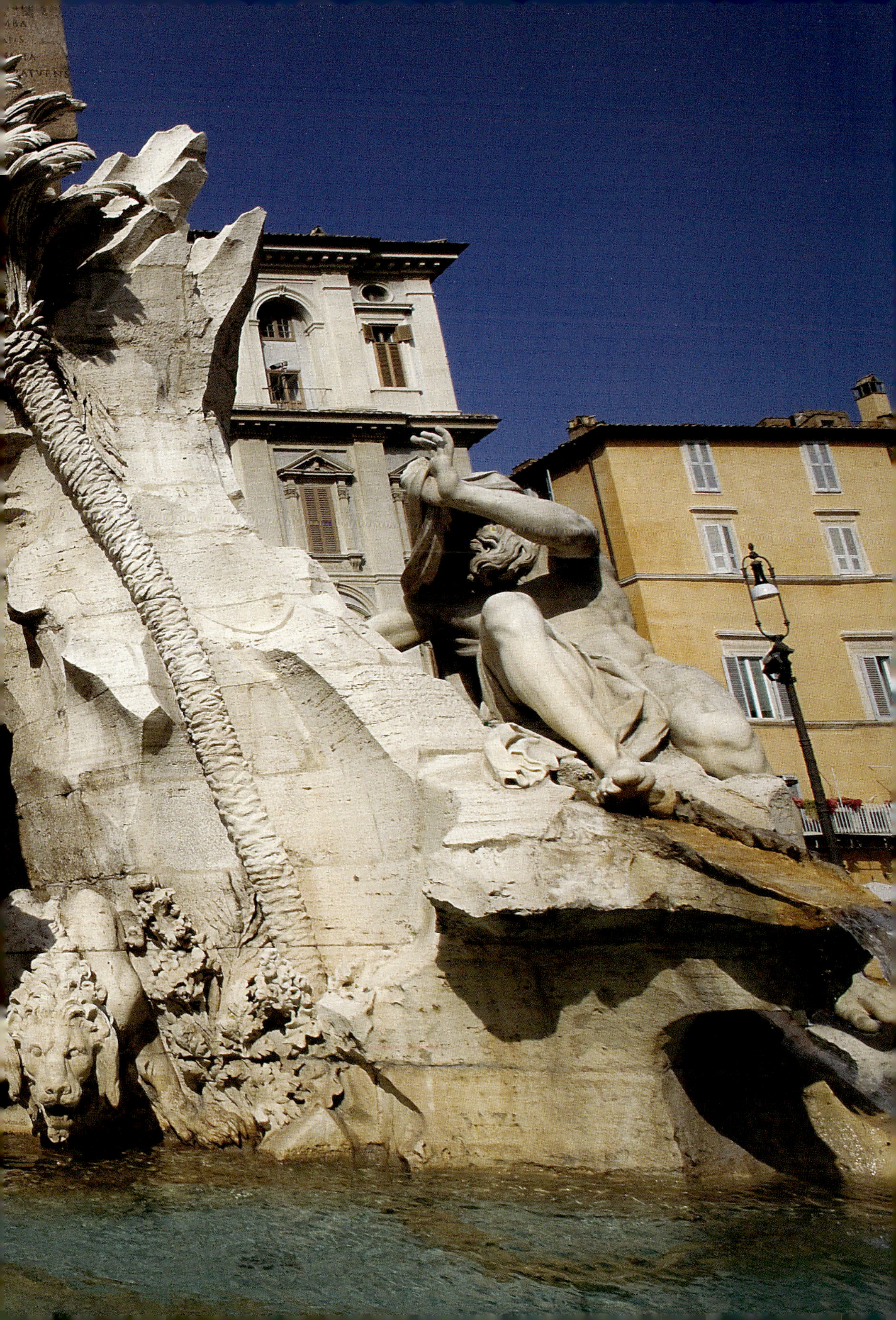

THE "BEL COMPOSTO": THE UNION OF THE ARTS

At the peak of his artistic career, in the works he created between the fifth and sixth decade of the 17th century, Bernini expressed his aesthetic ideal in a more accomplished manner, so well described by his son Domenico and by Baldinucci: "It is a matter of quite universal opinion that Bernini was the first artist to have attempted to unite architecture with sculpture and painting in such a way as to create a marvelous composite. He arrived at this state of perfection [...] by sometimes departing from the rules without, nonetheless, ever violating them, for his motto was "He who does not at times depart from the rule never exceeds it". Right from the first works, from the statues created for Villa Borghese, from *St Bibiana*, and the Baldacchino, Reliquary Balconies, and fountains, Bernini revealed his own personal, truly innovative and highly original conception, based on the relation between the work and the surrounding space and spectator.

Although he gave his supreme performance in the Cornaro Chapel (Fig. 29) in Santa Maria della Vittoria, Bernini fashioned a first example of an accomplished "bel composto", a fusion of architecture, sculpture, and painting, in the Raymondi Chapel in San Pietro in Montorio, dated to 1640-47. The chapel is dedicated to St Francis whose ecstasy is represented in bas-relief on the altar while sarcophaghi with busts of the deceased line the side-walls. The architectural and decorative scheme unifies the whole chapel: the architrave and decorative elements of the base run along the walls, the geometric motif is echoed in the pavement, and the altar relief is set into a concave surface that curves around to enclose the space naturally. Light from the two side windows floods the altar, heightening the mysticism of the ecstatic vision and creating a break between the worldly space intended for man and the celestial space of sanctity. On the walls, above the sarcophagi, whose occupants are being revealed by torch-bearing putti opening the lids, are the busts of the deceased, portrayed not in prayer or meditation, but in pleasant, natural attitudes, one reading a book, the other turning to the faithful and drawing them into the scenic space. The whiteness of the marble, another strongly unifying element bringing together the whole, is modulated by the richly carved surface contrasting with the ceiling, which is decorated with frescoes and gilt stuccoes featuring the *Glory of St Francis* in the centre.

Bernini left the execution of the work to his collaborators: Nicola Sale was responsible for the sarcophagi, Andrea Bolgi for the portraits and Francesco Baratta for the high altar relief. Baratta was born in Massa around 1600 and came to Rome in 1626 with Andrea Bolgi. We know little about his life and his artistic career was almost completely overshadowed by Bernini. Nevertheless, he was a

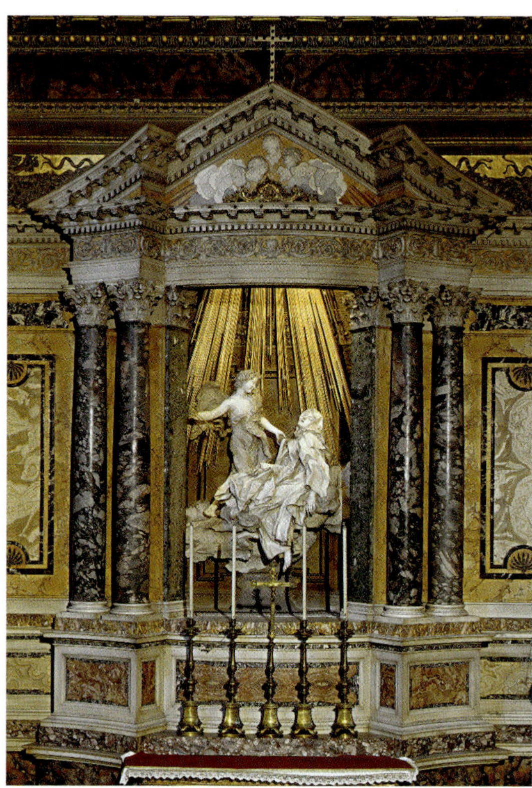

Fig. 29 (top) G. L. Bernini, *Cornaro Chapel* (1647-53), Rome, Church of Santa Maria della Vittoria.

Fig. 30 (right) G.L.Bernini, *Ecstasy of St Teresa of Avila* (c. 1649-50), Rome, Church of Santa Maria della Vittoria, Cornaro Chapel.

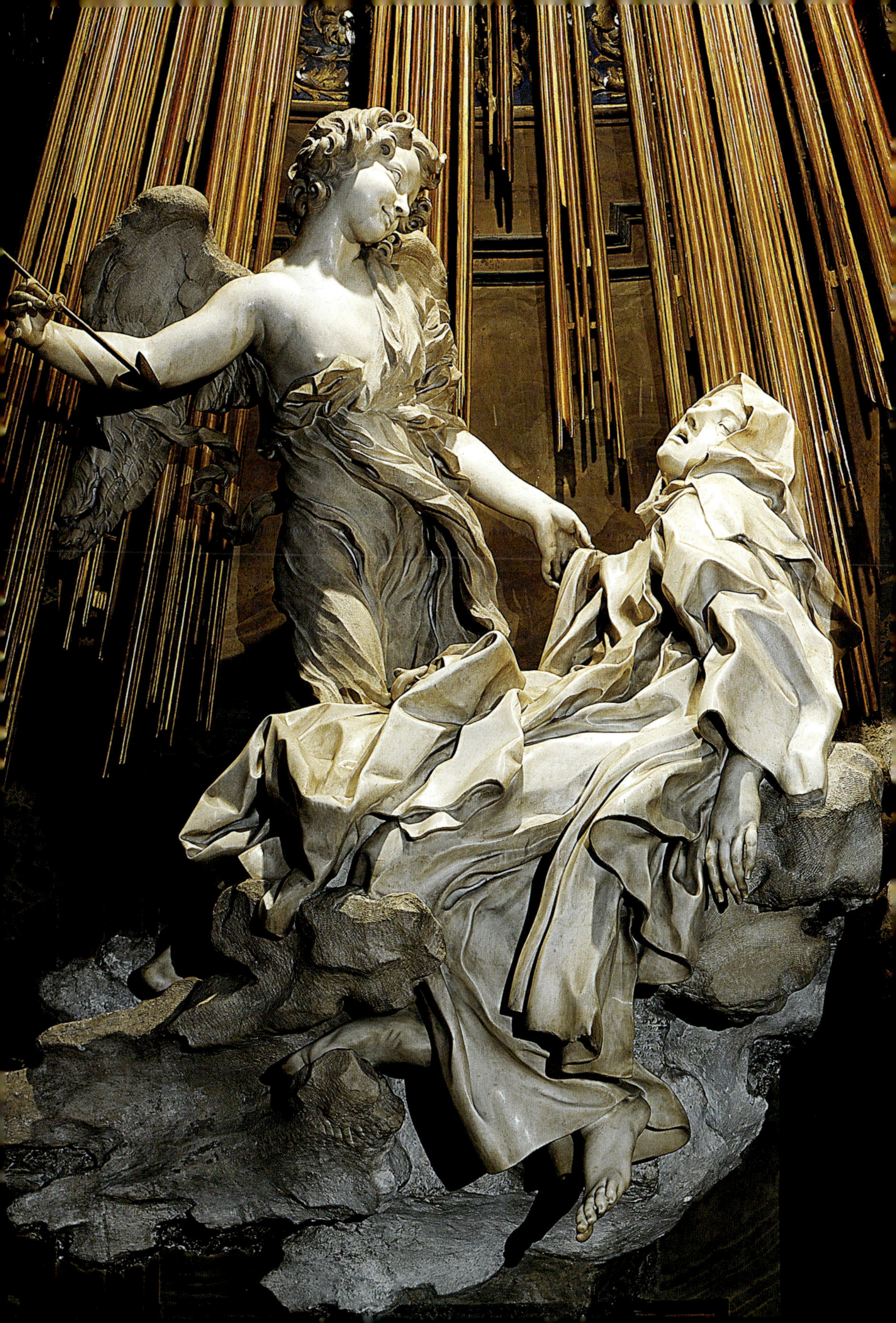

sculptor with a distinct personality: as well as working with his master on the Raymondi Chapel, he also worked with him on the nave of St Peter's, and on the *Fountain of the Four Rivers*, for which he executed the figure of the *Rio della Plata,* as well as on the *Fountain of the Moor*. The *Ecstasy of St Francis* relief reveals close ties to Bernini's stylistic approach, although it is softened by a gentler, more painterly type of modelling with a calmer language, which reins in the emotionally moving charge of the ecstatic vision.

The theme of ecstasy was particularly dear to the baroque sensibility, because it represented the highpoint of the yearning for the divine that so strongly characterised 17th-century religious sentiment. And in his *Ecstasy of St Teresa of Avila* (Fig. 30) for the Cornaro Chapel in Santa Maria della Vittoria, one of the supreme masterpieces of western art, Bernini showed that he was capable of depicting a sentiment as elusive, intimate and profound as ecstasy. In 1647, Cardinal Federico Cornaro, Knight of the Order of Malta, who had obtained the rights to the left transept of the church, commissioned Bernini to decorate the chapel (completed in 1652), which was to be dedicated to St Teresa, the great mystic, who was raised to the altars of sanctity in 1622. Bernini created a work that was complex yet unitary in the close relation linking every detail, every single decorative element, whether architectural, sculpted or painted, and consequential in its iconological and stylistic meanings, a dramatic spectacle that interprets baroque theatricality perfectly. The chapel is entirely faced with precious polychrome marbles and on the altar, which is enclosed in a lavish convex aedicule supported by three pillars, stands the white marble group of the saint who is lying back on a glory of clouds after being struck by the arrow of the angel standing alongside, while golden rays visualise the light descending from above. The saint is shown in the moment of abandonment to the sensation of ecstasy, sublime yet painful at once – as she herself wrote in her memoirs – her eyelids lowered, head thrown back, body wrapped in a rich gown whose swirling drapery folds around her body, underlining the strong emotions of her soul. Bernini adopts a purely theatrical conceit for the side walls by placing boxes decorated with black and yellow marble swags representing a pall where members of the Cornaro family are seated, watching the miraculous scene and discussing theology and the problem of transverberation (from the Latin *trasverberare*, that is, to pierce), which in the Catholic hagiography is the mystical experience attributed to a number of faithful injured by the supernatural intervention of God or angelic creatures. Looming above, a fresco of celestial glory; on the pavement below, inlaid marble skeletons, a frequent feature in Bernini's works, act as *memento mori.* Bernini succeeded in translating the miraculous scene of the vision into an image and in transmitting the emotion and profound affection of God's thought to the spectator. The faithful visiting the chapel cannot avoid being caught up in the miraculous event alongside the members of the Cornaro family, moved by the emotional state of abandonment of the body of St Teresa and entranced by the heavenly vision opening in the ceiling in an experience that will cause them to reflect upon their own end.

Together with his many collaborators, Bernini worked on the decorative schemes of numerous other chapels, from the De Sylva Chapel in the church of Sant'Isidoro (1660-63), with bas-relief portraits inserted into an opulent marble mantle, to the Fonseca Chapel in San Lorenzo in Lucina (1660-64) and the Albertoni Chapel in San Francesco a Ripa, executed during the papacy of Clement X, in 1671-74.

Fig. 31 (right)
Chigi Chapel Rome, Church of Santa Maria del Popolo.

THE REIGN OF ALEXANDER VII CHIGI

Although Bernini had fallen out of the pope's favour due to malicious rumours about the faulty design of the bell-towers of St Peter's, he soon made his comeback following the success of his *Fountain of the Four Rivers* and of the Cornaro Chapel in Santa Maria della Vittoria, and above all, the elevation of Alexander VII Chigi in 1655, plunging headlong into a range of activities. Alexander VII, an ambitious cultivated man and sophisticated patron, surrounded himself with the keenest intellects of the moment flanked by the leading artists – the like of Bernini, Borromini and Pietro da Cortona – with the aim of constructing *Roma Alexandrina.* He was particularly drawn to Bernini, calling upon him to carry out demanding new projects, both for sculptures and architectural programmes. The most important works executed by Bernini as sculptor for the Chigi pope were the Cathedra Petri, the Altar of the Holy Sacrament, the Scala Regia, the *Equestrian Statue of Constantine* in the Vatican basilica, the completion of the decorations in the

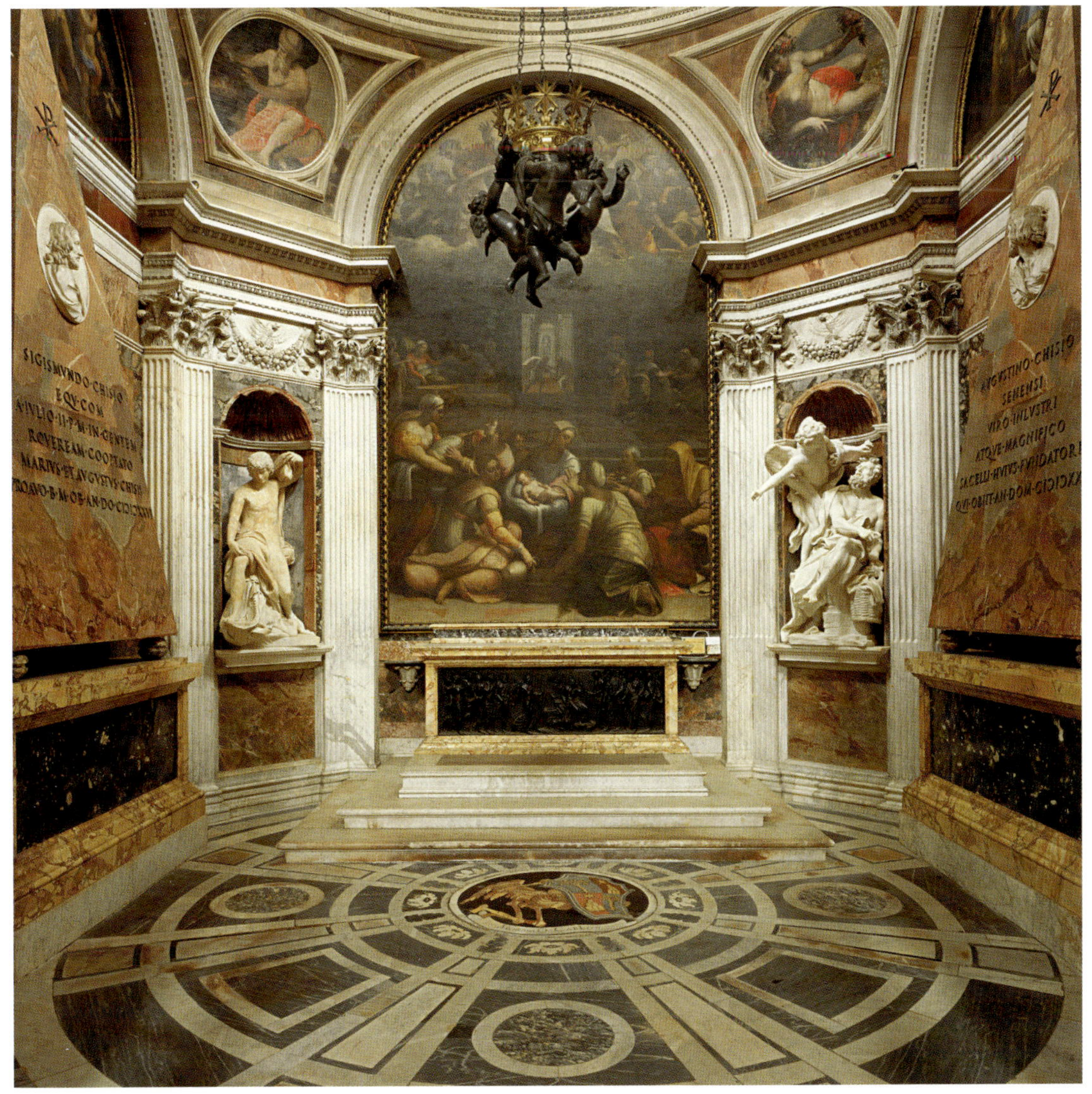

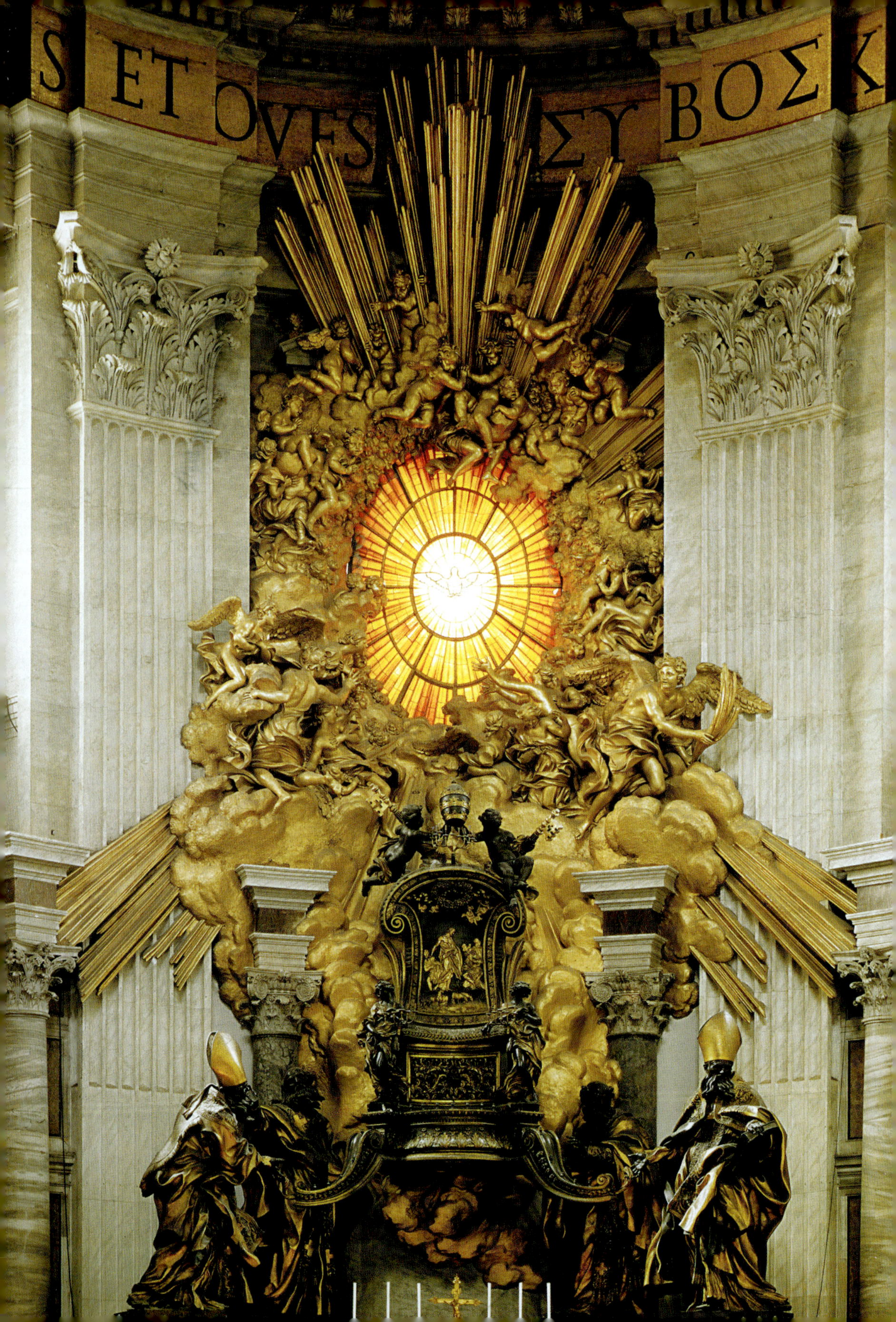
S ET OVES
ΣΥ ΒΟΣΚ

Chigi Chapel (Fig. 31) as well as the nave of the church of Santa Maria del Popolo and the Chigi Chapel in the Siena Duomo.

Yet again Bernini created works with a stunning impact on their site, sculptures capable of interacting with their surrounding space and creating focal points in the overall scenographic scheme. The *Cathedra Petri* (Fig. 32) is the work that best sums up his wholly baroque aesthetic ideal and his sense of scenographic drama, allowing us to fully understand this artist's creative method, his brilliant and profound sense of proportion and scenographic impact, and his ability to transform technical difficulties into strong points.

After setting up the Baldacchino and the Reliquary Balconies it became necessary to complete the arrangement of the apse space, whose decoration, begun under Urban VIII, had a long and complex history. In 1656 the decision was finally made to set up the ancient Chair of St Peter – which was actually from the early medieval period and had previously been displayed in the baptismal chapel – to underline the continuity of the figure of St Peter in the course of the centuries as well as the symbolic centrality of the figure of the pontiff, the apostle's spiritual heir. The following year, Alexander VII commmissioned Bernini to "execute" the work that would hold the much-venerated relic and that would keep the artist occupied for the next eleven years. The designs, bozzetti and models that have survived document the long genesis of Bernini's project, and reveal the artist's great sensitivity and attention to the spectacular effect produced by the work. As time went by the dimensions of the Cathedra (1656-1666) gradually expanded and the project became increasingly imposing: although the artist initially designed the work in proportion to the adjacent funerary monuments, he later adjusted the

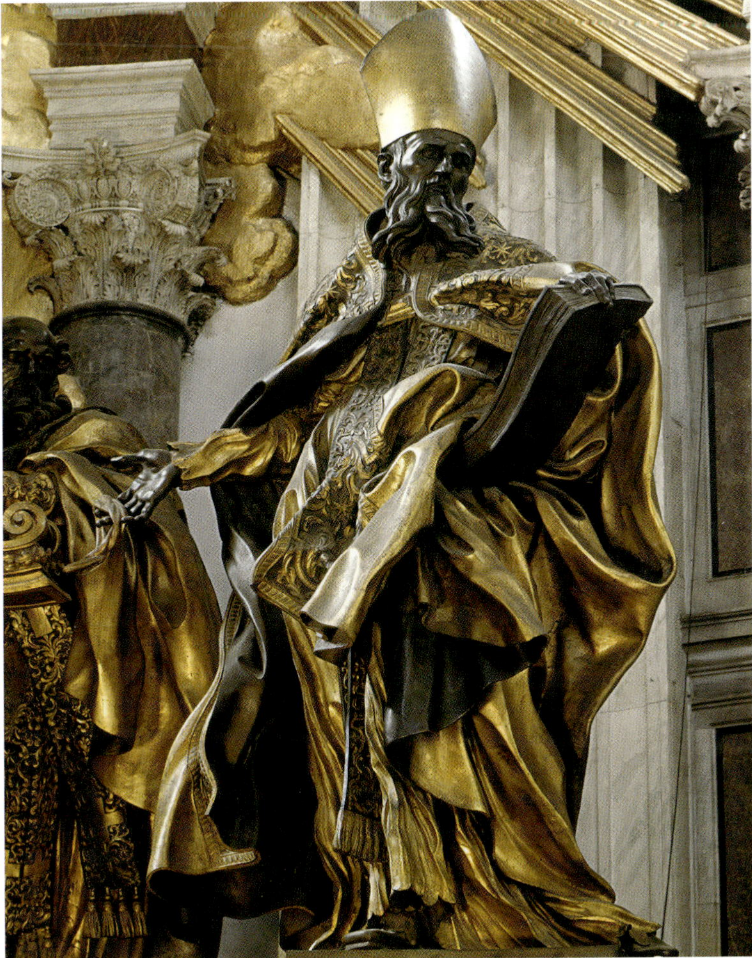

Fig. 32 (left)
G. L. Bernini,
Cathedra Petri (1656-66),
Vatican City,
St Peter's Basilica.

Fig. 33 (right)
G. L. Bernini,
Cathedra Petri,
detail of *St Augustine*
(1662-63), Vatican City,
St Peter's Basilica.

scale to the entire basilica with the aim of creating a focal point, the point of arrival of the faithful, after they have passed through long embrace of the church made tangible by the great colonnade in front of the basilica; during their approach they are faced with the view of the Chair framed by the Baldacchino, which functions as a canopy for the high altar as well as proscenium arch, giving the setting an distinctly scenographic theatrical appearance. The bronze cathedra, which encloses the ancient wooden chair, is decorated with reliefs depicting stories from the Life of St Peter and is supported on its upward flight by the four doctors of the church: *St Augustine* (Fig. 33) and *St Ambrose* (Fig. 34) of the Western Church, and *St Athanasius* and *St John Chrysostom* of the Eastern Church. Their emphatic gestures, harmonious attitudes, and bulky drapery expanding in space cause the four figures appear intensely expressive. The Cathedra ascends towards celestial glory, a dizzying explosion of clouds and angels encircling the dove set in the centre of the window, from which a golden light descends.

This monumental work entailed a huge commitment in terms of the expense involved in procuring such vast quantities of bronze, the technical skills involved in fusion, and the work resulting from the colossal dimensions of the Cathedra – considering that the figures of the doctors are over five metres high. Bernini was forced to call upon a large group of collaborators, many of whom distinguished themselves, including Ercole Ferrata, Antonio Raggi and Lazzaro Morelli.

The Chigi epoch ended with the *Monument to Alexander VII* (Fig. 35), which was executed some years after the death of the pope, between 1671 and 1678. By now aged almost eighty, Bernini only delivered the designs, while the monument was actually executed by his assistants, who included Michele Maglia, Lazzaro Morelli, Giuseppe Mazzuoli and Giulio Cartari. Nonetheless the work draws upon a typically Berniniesque language, yet again revealing Bernini's creativity and inventiveness in resolving practical problems and transforming them into innovative solutions. The monument was to be placed in the niche in the south transept, which held a passageway leading to a series of rooms. Bernini draped a bulky swag of Sicilian jasper over the doorway that resembled the drapery used for the *Monument to Blessed Ludovica Albertoni* in the Altieri Chapel – a highly scenographic and prominent feature raised up by a skeleton holding up an hourglass, thus transforming an ordinary doorway into a symbolic passageway to the true tomb of the pope and into the entrance to the afterlife.

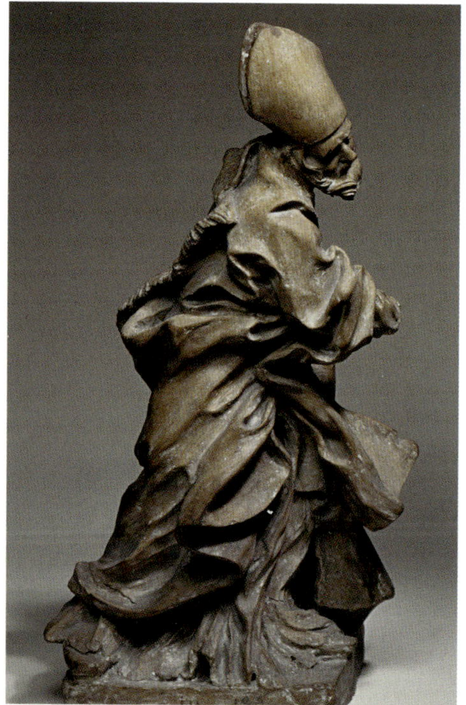

Fig. 34 (left)
G. L. Bernini,
Bozzetto for the figure of St Ambrose
(1662-63), St Petersburg,
Hermitage Museum.

Fig. 35 (right)
G. L. Bernini and helpers,
Monument to Alessandro VII
(1671-78), Vatican City, St Peter's Basilica.

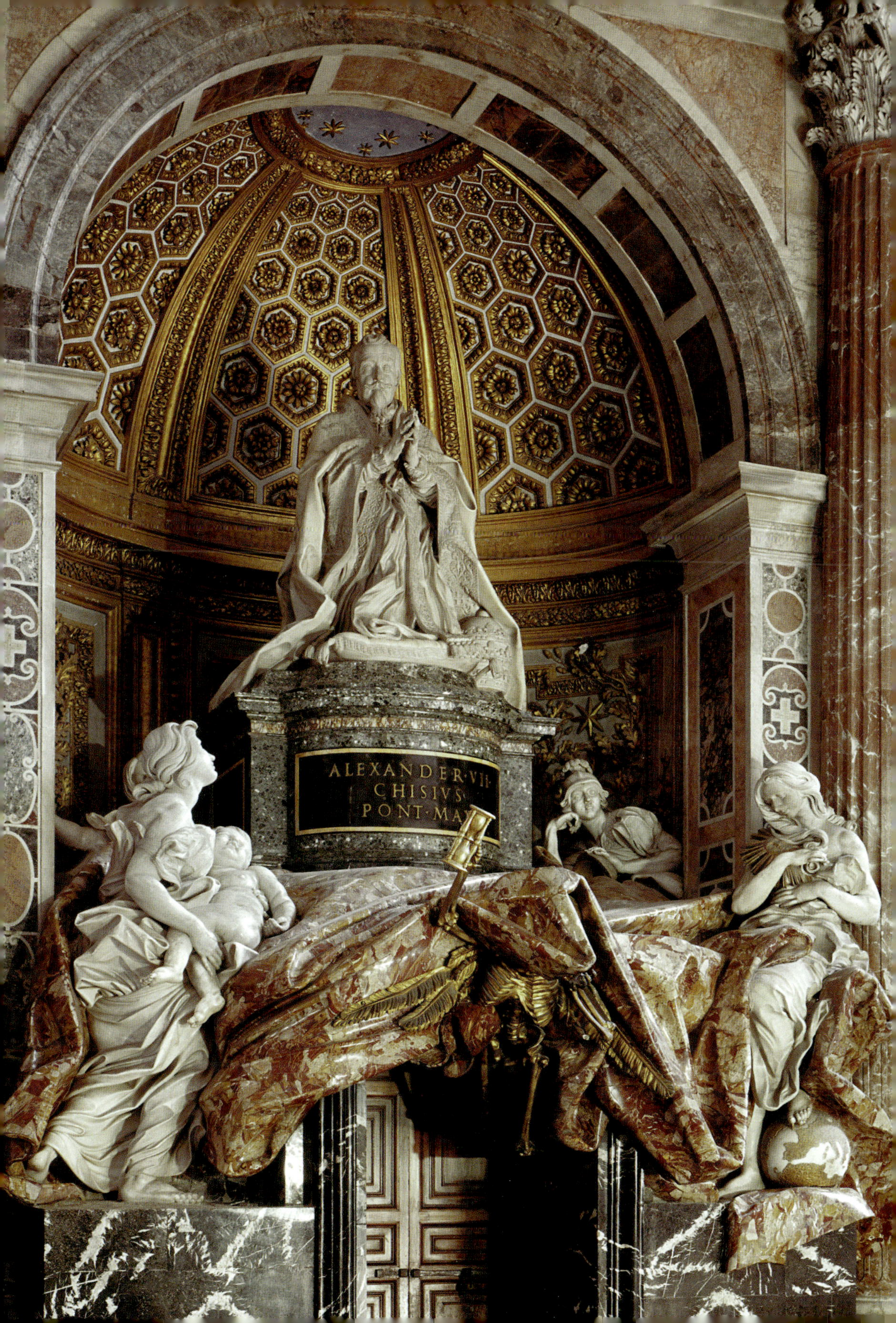
ALEXANDER·VII·
CHISIVS
PONT·MA

THE LATE BERNINI

Around the seventh decade of the 17th century, Bernini's style, previously characterised by formal exuberance and, at the same time, an incredible grasp of reality, began to change direction, turning towards a more expressionist form that would gradually intensify in time. This new style probably reflects the artist's deepening religious sentiment and his changing vision of life. The texts that he was constantly reading – the *Imitation of Christ* by Thomas à Kempis and *Introduction to the Devout Life* by St Francis of Sales – his frequent religious practices, going to mass every day, his encounters with religious men like Padre Oliva, the Jesuit General Superior, with whom a deep friendship grew up – reveal a devotion that appeared in the artist's mature years and that intensified in old age, confirmed by his biographers, Filippo Baldinucci and Domenico Bernini as well as, above all, by his works.

The sculptures that Bernini executed during the final years of his life gradually acquired an increasingly heightened and dramatic sense of emotion, and exaggerated dynamism, a less natural and more expressionist language in a crescendo that left everyone astonished. In fact, amazement is the only possible reaction when faced with the gallery of works from his final years: they include the doctors of the Cathedra, the *St Jerome* in the Chigi Chapel in the Siena Duomo, the *Portrait Bust of Gabriele Fonseca* in the church of San Lorenzo in Lucina, the *Angels* on the Ponte Sant'Angelo, the *Blessed Ludovica Albertoni*, but also religious drawings (like *St Jerome Adoring the Cross* and the *Magdalene Kneeling in Adoration of the Cross*), or even sacred furnishings as in the tabernacle of the Collegiate Church of the Assunta at Ariccia, which bears a depiction of a chalice with a host surrounded by flames symbolising mystic ardour. Bernini's spirituality is summed up in an engraving that he executed in the final years of his life, *The Sea of Blood*, showing St Maria Maddalena dei Pazzi kneeling to collect the blood flowing from the wounds of the crucified Christ, the sole source of the salvation of humanity.

Although, as we have seen, Bernini abandoned his "speaking likeness" to create the "ideal likeness" for Francesco I and Louis XIV as early as 1650, his two sculptures depicting *St Jerome* and *St Mary Magdalene* in the Chigi Chapel of the Duomo of Siena mark yet another watershed in his art. The hollow-eyed St Jerome, his intensely devout expression and the gesture he makes as he brings the Crucifix and drapery to his face all bear witness to and amplify the saint's emotional state and feelings. The transformation undergone by Bernini emerges with even greater clarity if one compares his 1624 *St Bibiana* to the 1662 *St Mary Magdalene*: here the saint is shown standing up straight, leaning against a column, her ecstatic face is turned upwards, one hand raised and the other lowered to hold the palm of martyrdom. The rippling drapery of the gown creates a chromatic impact due to the continuous passage from shade to light caused by the deep folds. In his *St Mary Magdalene*, the drapery does not lie against her contorted body but billows with the saint's emotions, and her expression is no longer one of sweet ecstasy but one of inner torment.

Bernini's expressionism reached its peak with two works sculpted between 1668 and 1674: the *Portrait Bust of Gabriele Fonseca* (Fig. 36) in the chapel of the same name in San Lorenzo in Lucina and the *Blessed Ludovica Albertoni* in San Francesco a Ripa. The portrait of the Physician Fonseca, who is shown leaning out of the frame containing his bust, represents Bernini at the summit of his passionate, sentimental and touching art. Fonseca's face, which is contorted and furrowed with the pain of contrition, his hand pressed against his chest in an instinctive movement, and his drapery in disordered folds, causes the work to arouse strong emotions in the viewer. Even more moving is Bernini's sculpture of the *Blessed Ludovica Albertoni* (Fig. 37). The nun, who is lying on a bed, is in the throes of a mystical vision so strong that it

Fig. 36 (right)
G. L. Bernini,
Portrait of Gabriele Fonseca (1668-72),
Rome, Church of San Lorenzo in Lucina.

Fig. 37 (overleaf)
G. L. Bernini, *Monument to the Blessed Ludovica Albertoni* (1674), Rome,
Church of San Francesco a Ripa.

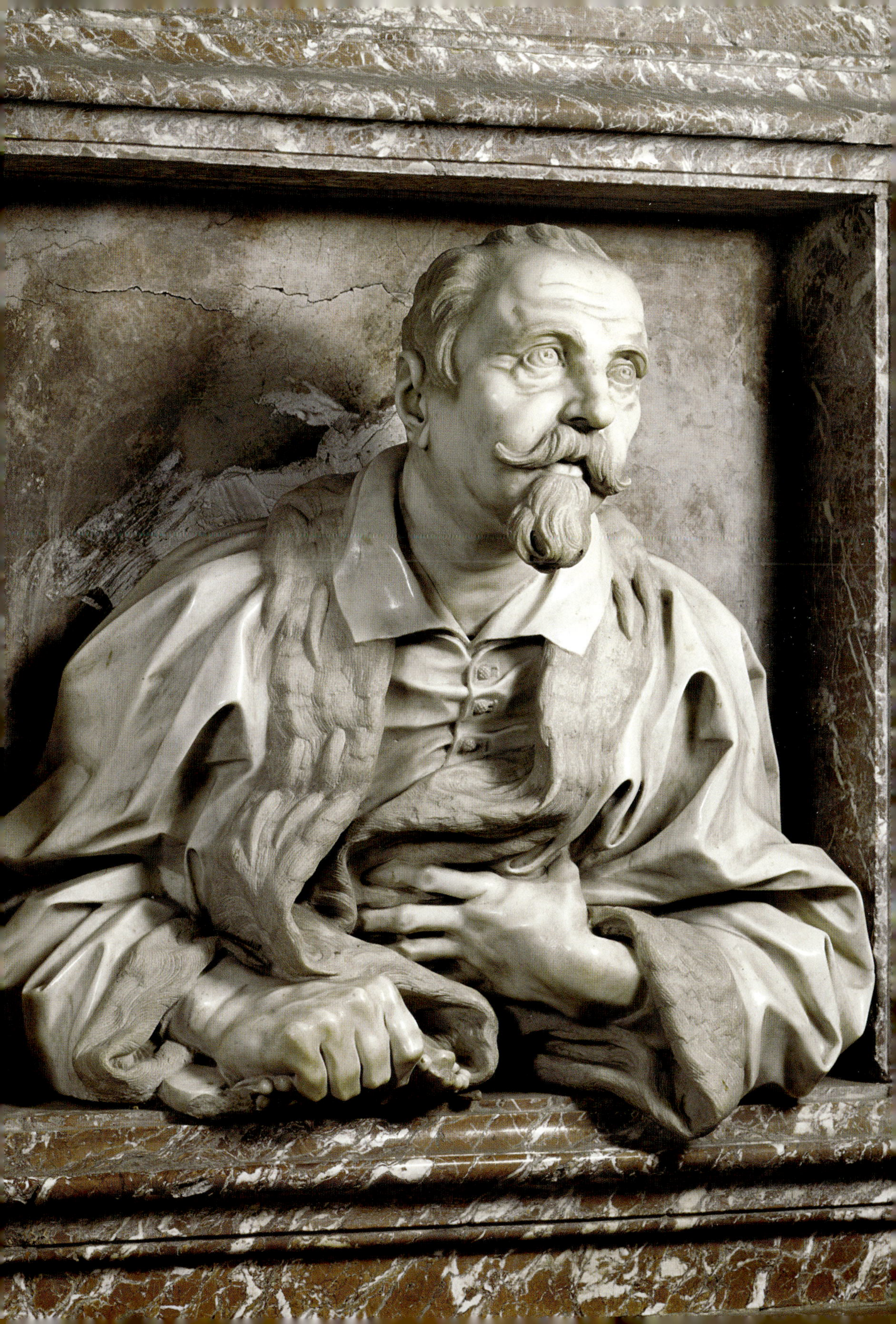

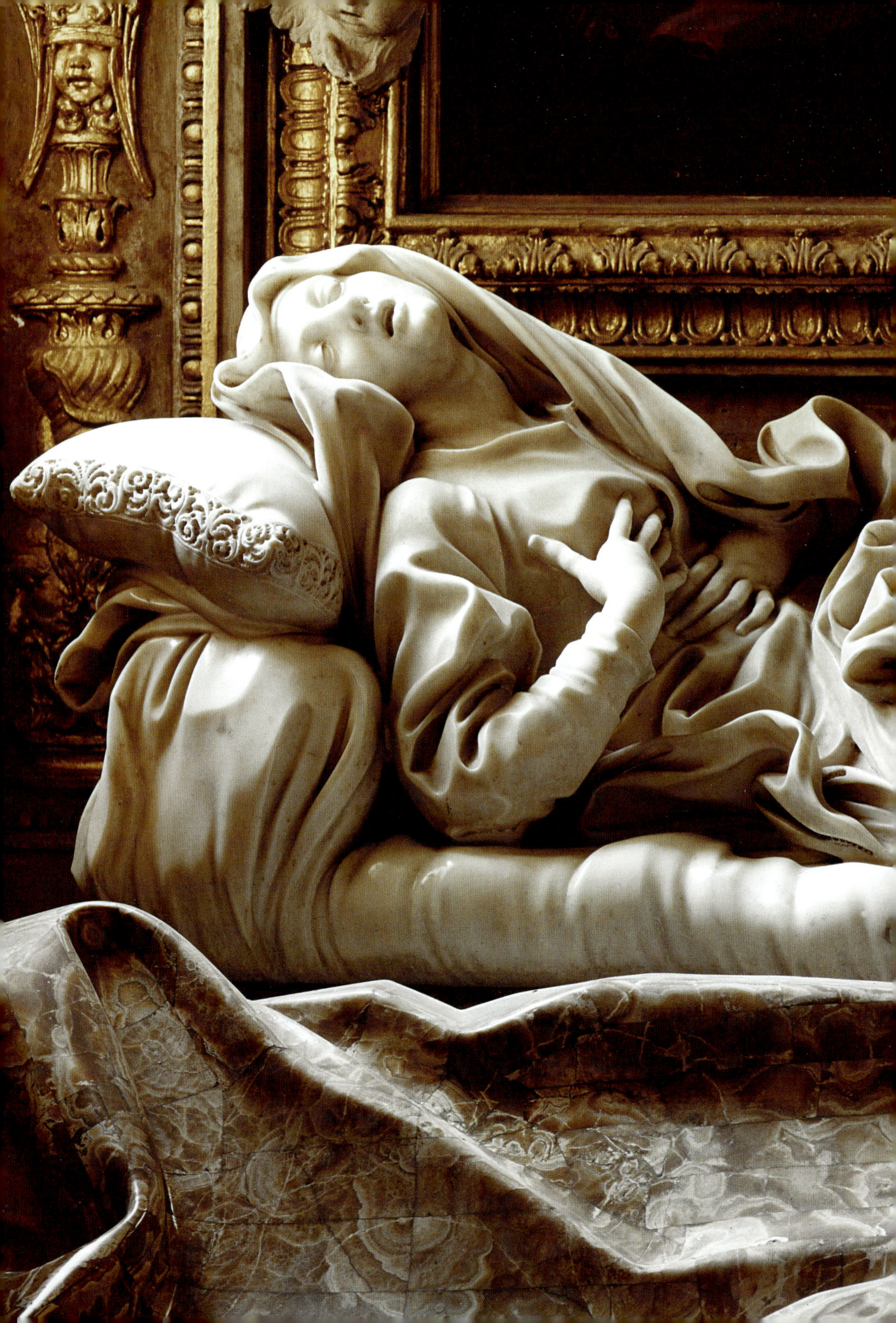

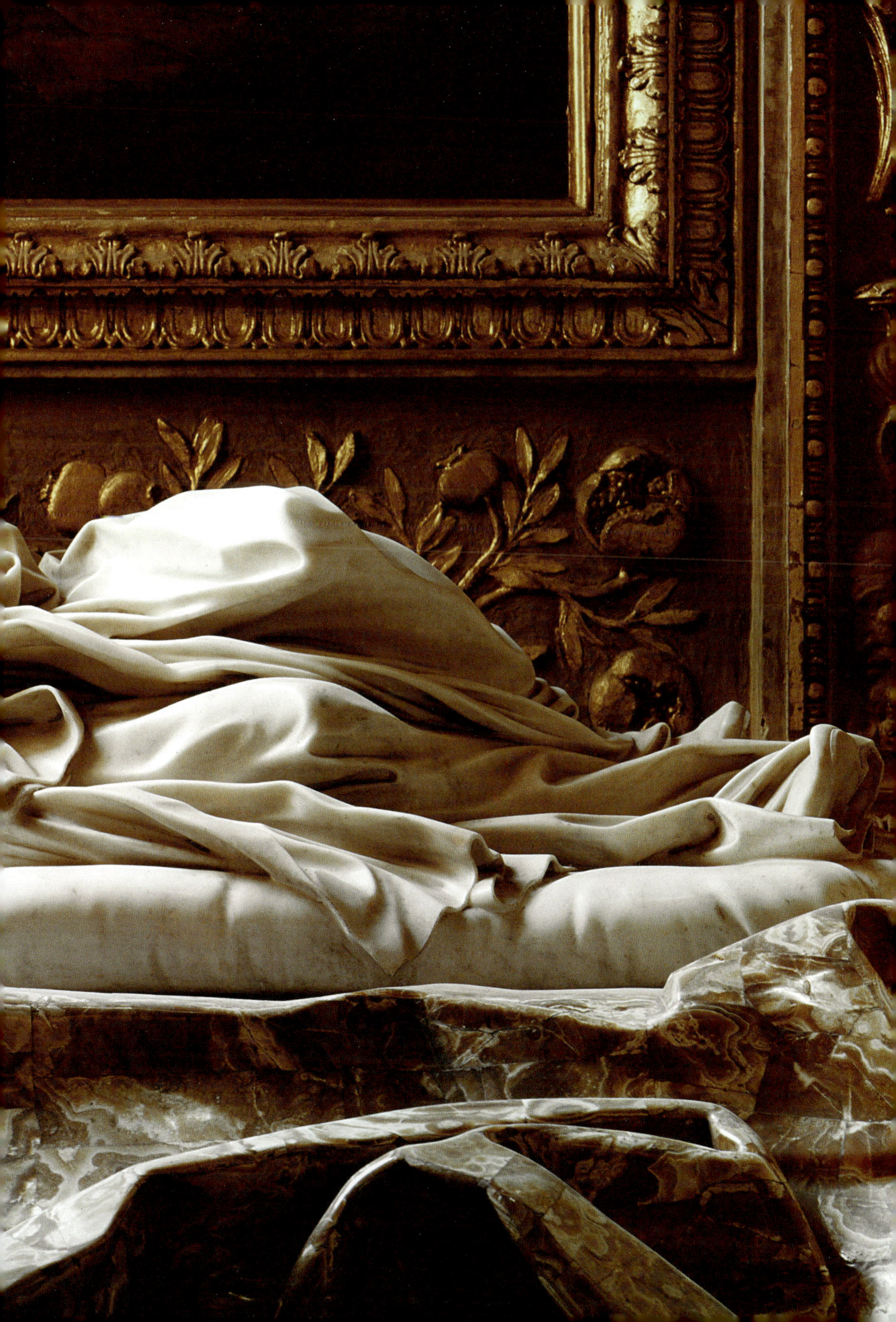

causes her body to arch; the rich drapery of her gown and her huge jasper pall heighten the drama of the scene. The writings of St Teresa of Avila, the other mystical saint whom Bernini was familiar with after dedicating the Cornaro Chapel to her, help us to understand Albertoni's feelings at the time of the ecstatic rapture: "Do not think, daughters, that it is an exaggeration to say that the soul is dying. That is indeed what is happening, because, as I have already told you, love operates with such force at times that it seizes control of all human faculties".

The decoration of the *Ponte Sant'Angelo* (Fig. 38) was launched under Clement IX with ten figures of angels bearing the symbols of the Passion of Christ. The arrangement of this bridge was of great strategic importance, because it represented the only access route to the basilica of St Peter's for those arriving from the north. Pope Clement wished to create a sa-

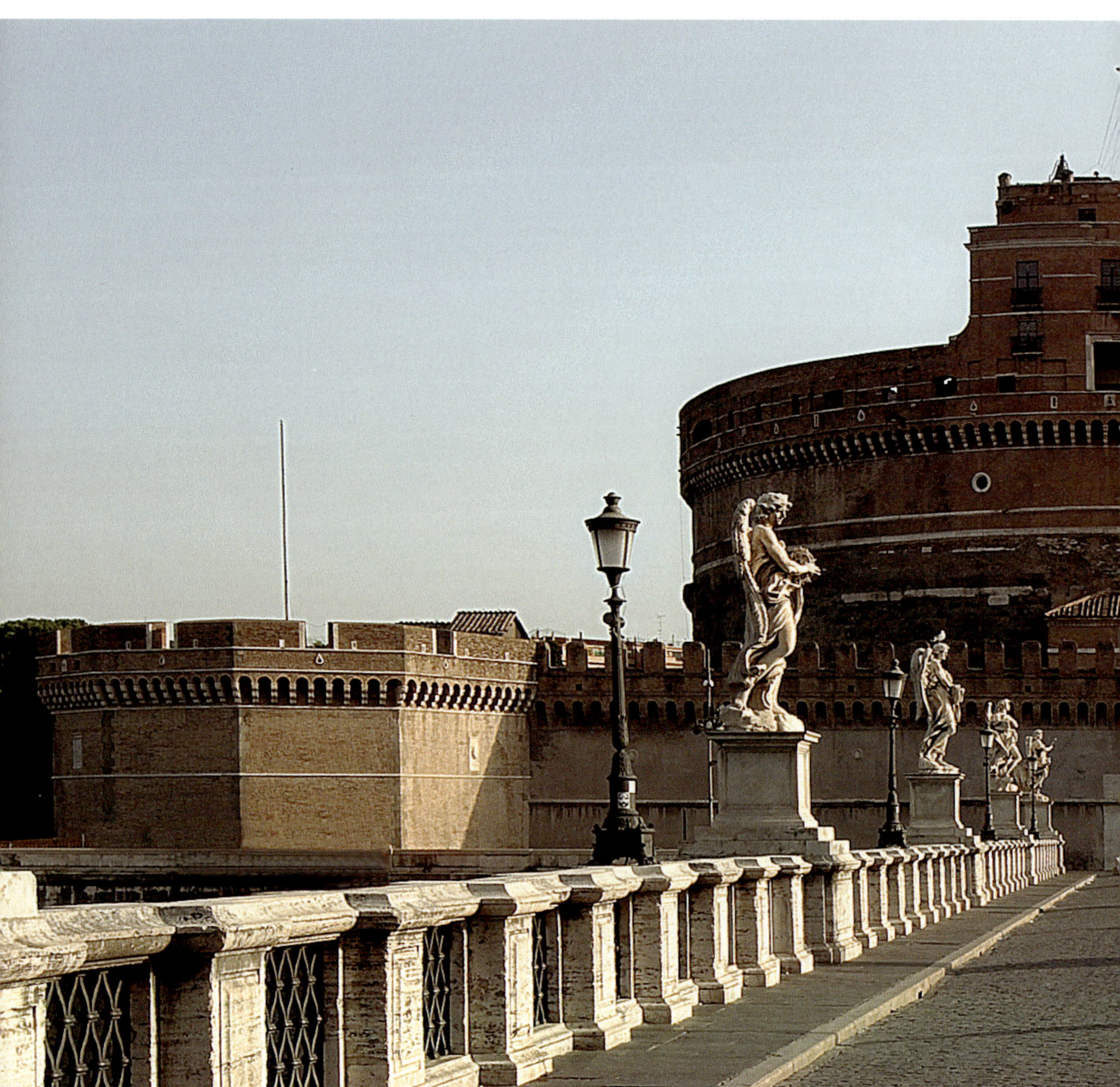

Fig. 38 Ponte Sant'Angelo (1667-69), Rome.

cred path for pilgrims approaching the greatest temple of Christianity, starting at the bridge, where the angels would have inspired a reflection on the Passion of Christ in a personal journey of purification, continuing in the great colonnade of the basilica, which symbolised the embrace of the Church, and then concluding in the interior of the sacred building where, drawn by the Baldacchino, pilgrims would continue their journey of faith towards the altar of St Peter and celestial glory, symbolised by the whirling clouds and angels above the Cathedra.

The master executed two angels in person, the *Angel with the Superscription of the Cross* (Figs. 39-40) and the *Angel with the Crown of Thorns*. When he saw the beauty and outstanding quality of the two statues, Clement IX did not wish them to be placed on the bridge to be exposed to the elements, so Bernini kept them in his studio (where they remained until the

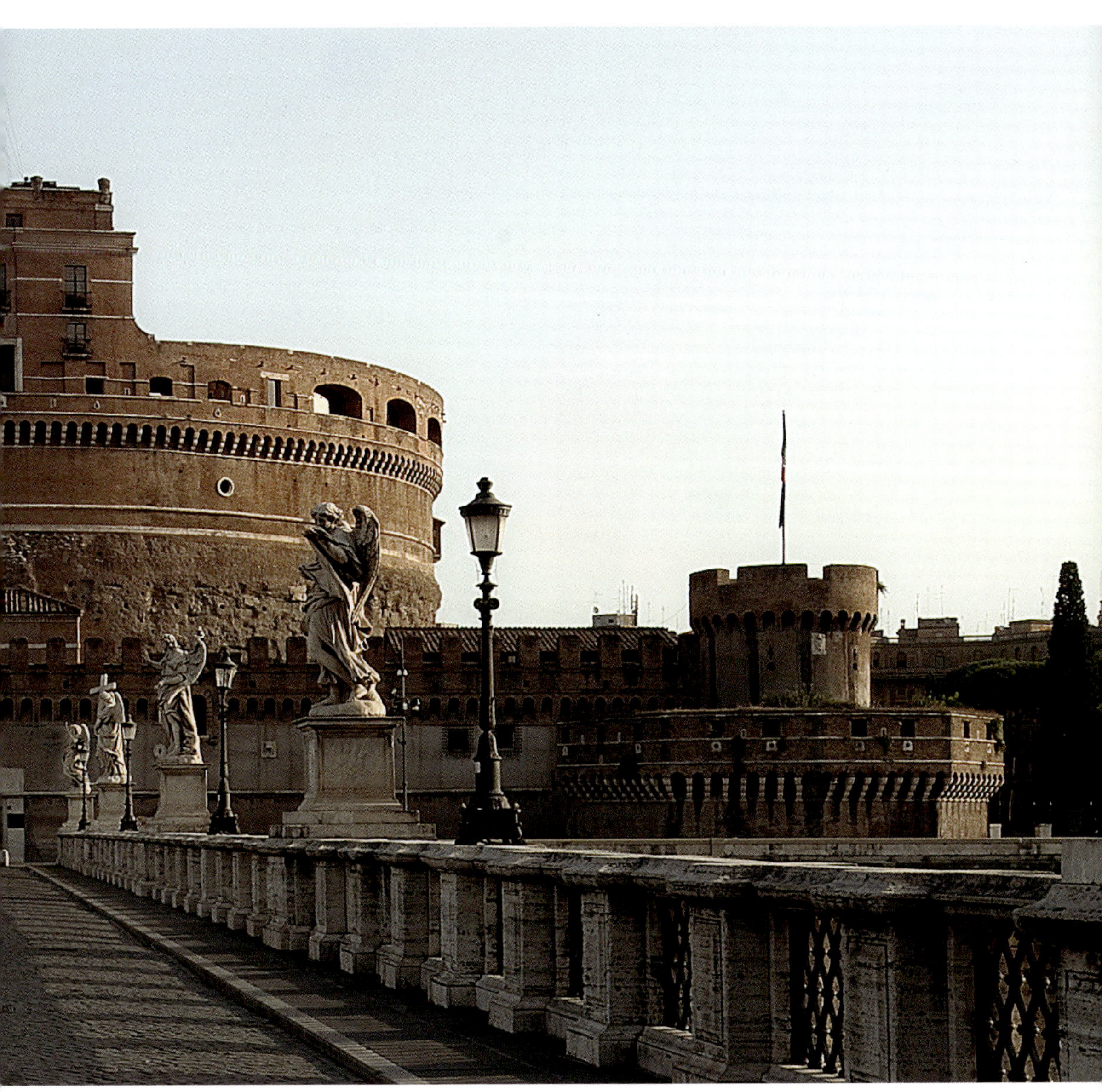

early 18th century, when they were moved to the church of Sant'Andrea delle Fratte), and entrusted the execution of the sculptures to a group of his assistants, supplying them with designs and bozzetti. Lazzaro Morelli carved the *Angel with the Scourge;* Girolamo Lucenti, the *Angel with the Nails*; Paolo Naldini, the *Angel with the Garments and Die*; Antonio Giorgetti, the *Angel with the Sponge*; Domenico Guidi, the *Angel with the Lance*; Cosimo Fancelli, the *Angel with the Veil*; Ercole Ferrata, the *Angel with the Cross*; Antonio Raggi, the *Angel with the Column*; and Paolo Naldini the *Angel with the Crown of Thorns.* According to Baldinucci, Bernini was unwilling that "a work [...] to which he felt so obliged should lack some work of his own hand" personally intervened upon the *Angel with the Superscription of the Cross* by sculpting the second version of the original sculpture now in the church of Sant'Andrea delle Fratte.

The group of Angels is distinguished by a uniform style because the maestro supplied his assistants with sketches and terracotta bozzetti basically repeating the same pose in all the statues: the angels all have wavy locks, their bodies are enveloped in rich drapery leaving one leg and one shoulder uncovered while their great wings are folded.

The striking bridge parapets were designed by Bernini himself who inserted metal grilles into the sides to afford passersby a pleasant view of the waters flowing in the river below. As Bernini mentioned on several occasions, he was a "friend of water" and susceptible to its charms. According to his biographers, the last sculpture to be made by Bernini was the *Bust of the Saviour* that he carved in honour of Queen Christina of Sweden. In his biography of his father, Domenico describes its creation with the following words: "However, approaching the time of his death and at the advanced age of eighty, the Cavaliere wished to bring honour to his life and bring to termination the practice of his profession thus far so well conducted with the creation of a work of such a nature that truly fortunate can we reckon that man who thereby ends his days. The work in question was

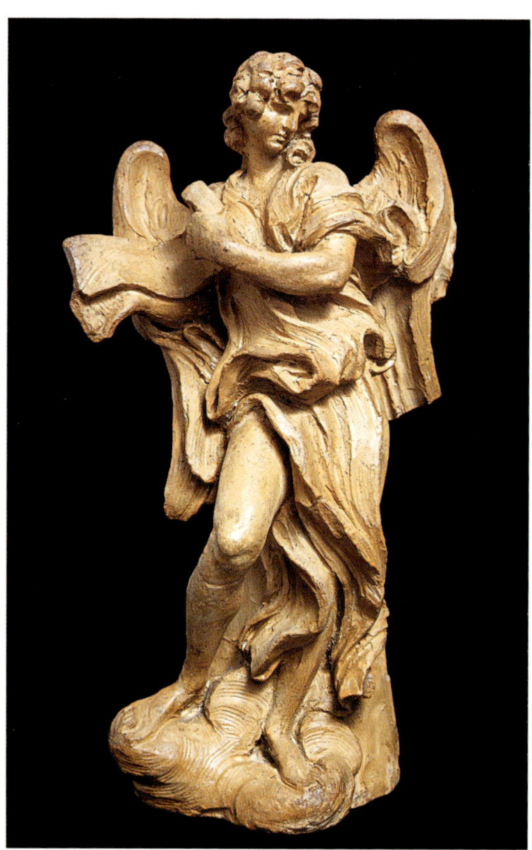

Fig. 39 G. L. Bernini,
Angel with the Superscription of the Cross
(1667-68), bozzetto, Rome,
Museo Nazionale del Palazzo Venezia.

an image of our Saviour in half-figure [...] with his right hand slightly raised, as if in the act of imparting a blessing". The work has been lost but this detailed description has made it possible to identify two later copies of Bernini's *Salvator Mundi*, one in a museum in Norfolk, Virginia, another in the basilica of San Sebastiano fuori le Mura in Rome. However, these two sculptures cannot be attributed to the hand of the master because they lack that throbbing emotional touch that made Bernini the greatest sculptor of his time, that incomparable ability to model the marble and instil it with life, spirit, soul, and emotions that would continue to characterise even the works of his final period.

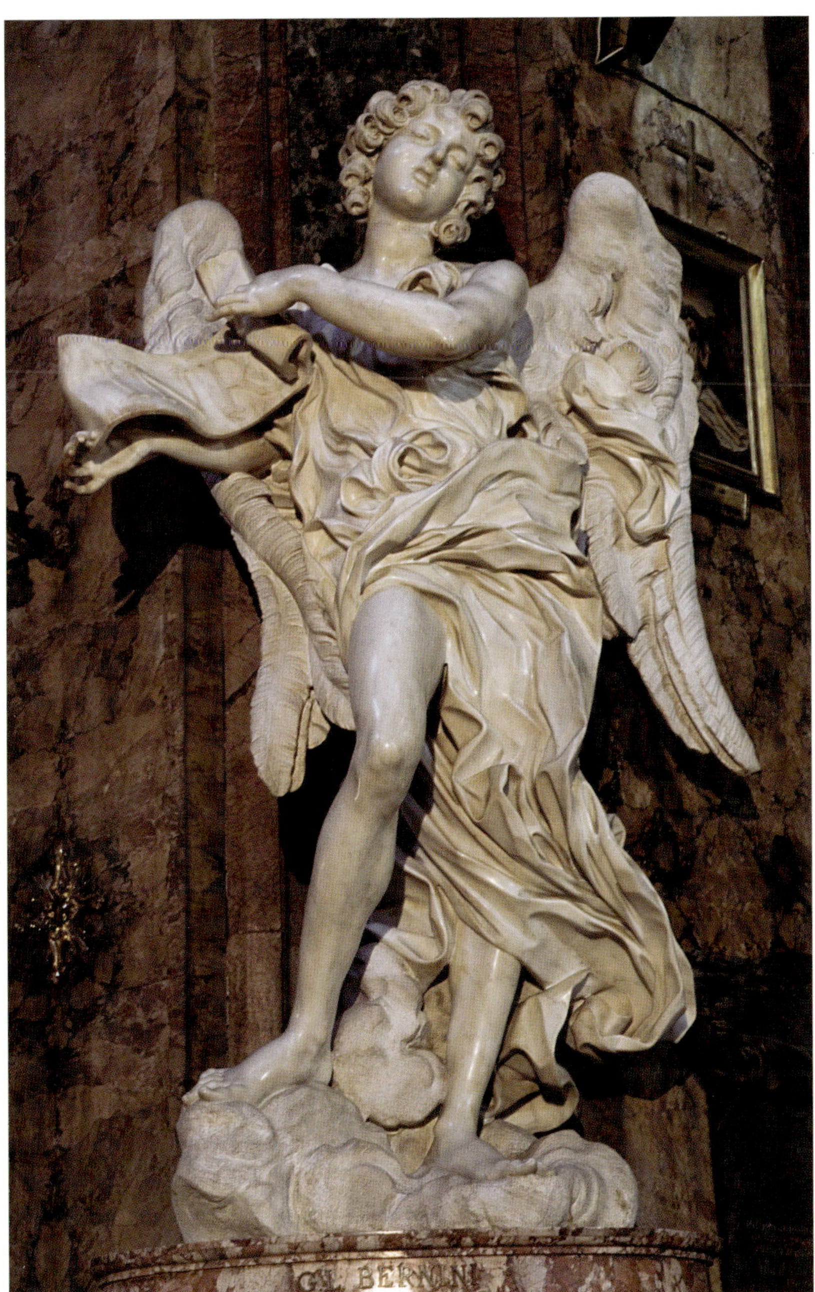

Fig. 40
G. L. Bernini,
Angel with the Superscription of the Cross
(1668-69), Rome,
Church of Sant'Andrea delle Fratte.

PUPILS, ASSISTANTS AND FOLLOWERS

In 17th-century Rome, all the leading sculptural and architectural undertakings were directed by Gian Lorenzo Bernini. Such was the complexity and scale of these works that he obviously required considerable assistance from his collaborators. Even in his earliest youthful works Bernini worked with helpers. When executing his *St Bibiana* and his *Apollo and Daphne* group, Bernini called upon Giuliano Finelli who brought incredible technical skill to his execution of details like Daphne's feet transforming into roots or her wind-blown hair. An entire retinue of sculptors and stone masons worked on the construction of the Baldacchino in St Peter's: Francesco Borromini, who was probably responsible for the covering of the vast structure, François Duquesnoy, Giuliano Finelli, Andrea Bolgi, Stefano Speranza, Jacopo Antonio Fancelli, Luigi Bernini and Nicolò Sale.

Most 17th-century sculptors were involved to a greater or lesser degree in the workshop set up by Bernini around the 1640s, resulting in the widespread diffusion of a Berniniesque style, especially in the second half of the century.

As mentioned above, the colossal works commissioned from Bernini required the collaboration of a large retinue of assistants with whom he had very different relationships: those working for him included Borromini and Algardi who can hardly be defined his pupils, while others, like Andrea Bolgi, participated in many of his projects without ever fully assimilating his language and adopting more measured, calmer stylistic approaches; some, like Ferrata, a former pupil of Algardi, worked in Bernini's workshop and were numbered among his closest collaborators, while others, like Antonio Raggi, were totally faithful to the master. Even when numerous helpers were involved or when the master's participation was limited to the design phase, Bernini's projects were always distinguished by a stylistic uniformity resulting from the original creative power of his ideas. We must not forget that Bernini participated to various degrees in his different works: in some he contributed the drawings as well as working in person, in others he called upon numerous assistants, and in yet others he contributed only the design.

For example, he worked on the Baldacchino without interruption for at least three years while for the *Fountain of the Four Rivers* he entrusted the allegorical figures of the rivers to his pupils and reserved the execution of the central rock formation for himself; for the project for Ponte Sant'Angelo he entrusted

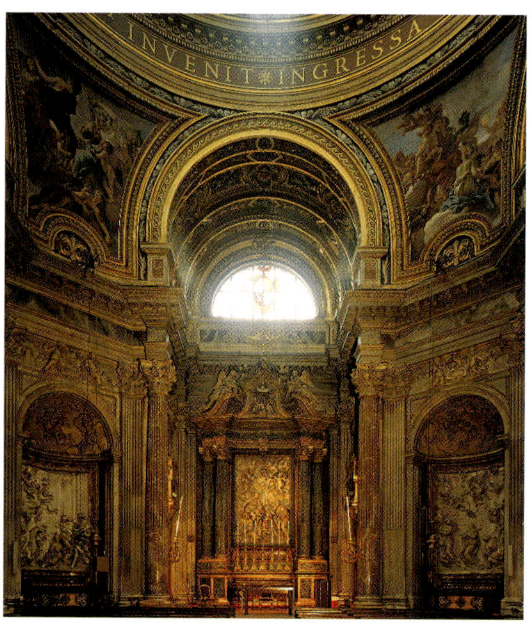

Fig. 41 (left)
Rome, Church of Sant'Agnese in Agone, interior.
Right altar: Ercole Ferrata,
Martydrom of St Emerentiana (1660-68),
relief completed by Leonardo Retti in 1709;
left altar: Antonio Raggi,
Death of St Cecilia (1662-65).

Fig. 42 (right)
Ercole Ferrata,
Martydrom of St Emerentiana (1660-68),
detail, Rome, Church of Sant'Agnese in Agone.

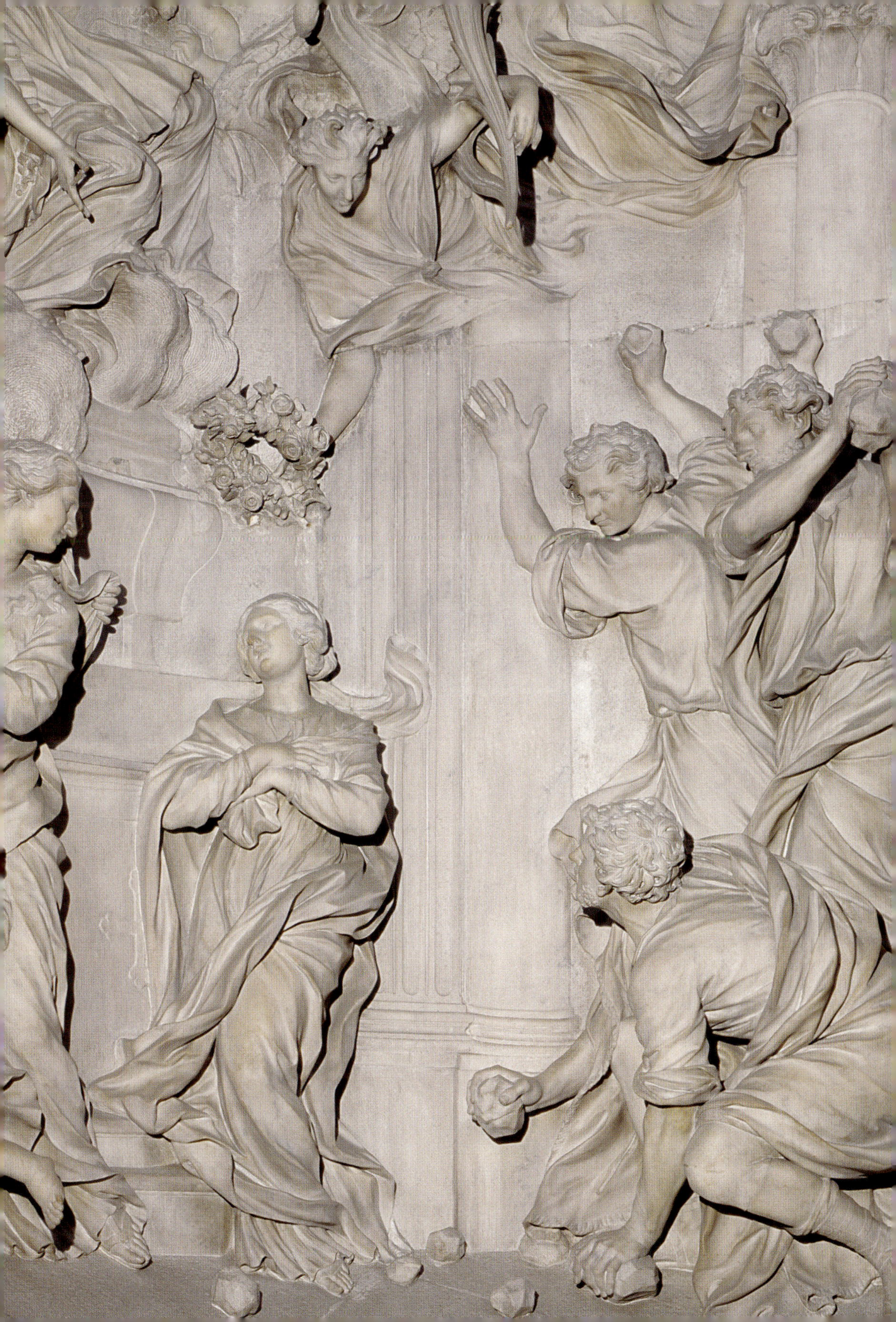

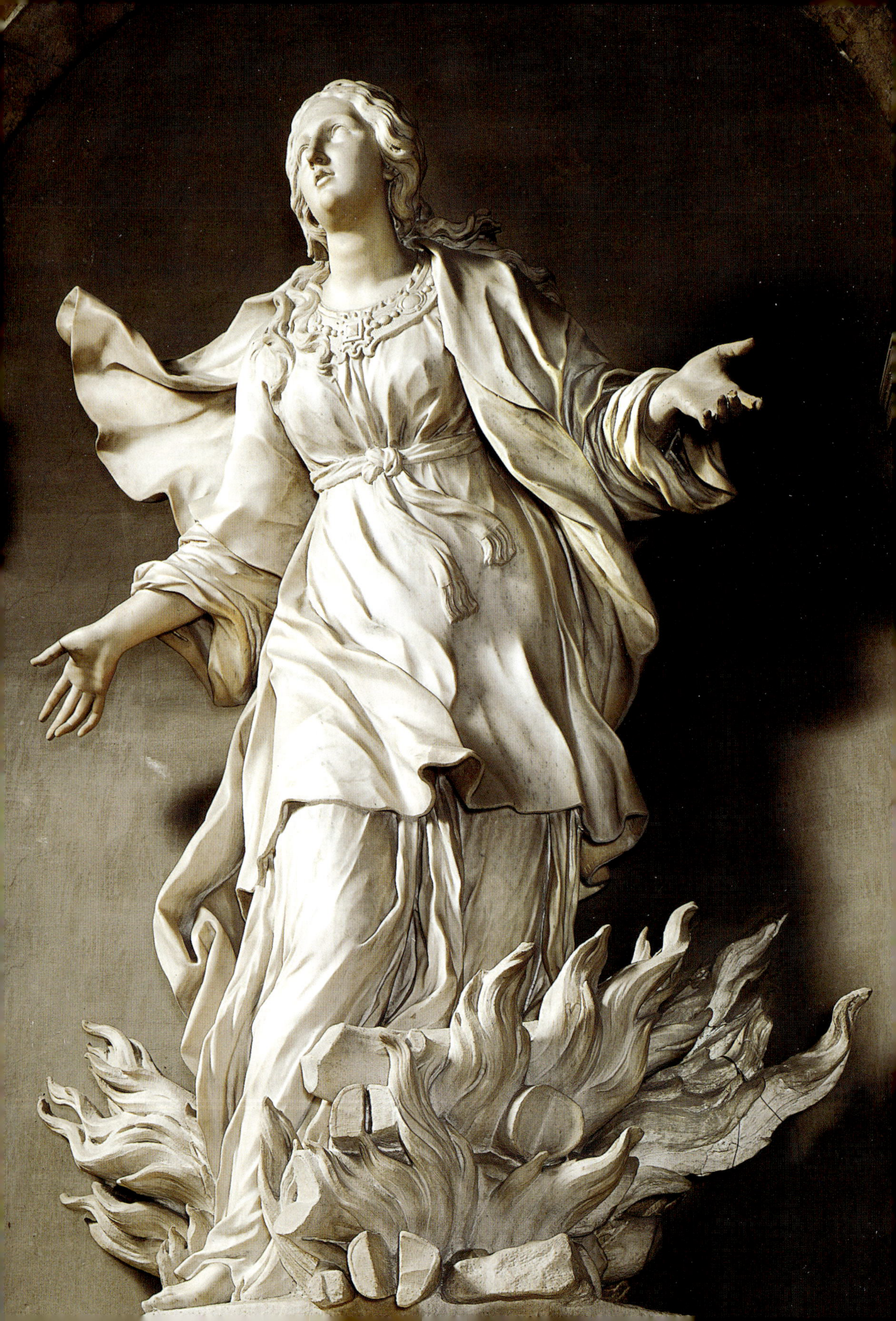

all the sculptures to his pupils, carving only the *Angel with the Superscription of the Cross* (apart from the two angels now in Sant'Andrea delle Fratte); the *Monument to Alexander VII* was entirely the work of his assistants, although Bernini supplied the designs and probably intervened during the final phase.

Although Bernini dominated the Roman art scene during the first half of the 17th century, he was flanked by sculptors of the calibre of Algardi, Mochi and Duquesnoy, who maintained their own idiosyncratic style, while during the second half of the century, artists tended to adopt a Berniniesque vocabulary and more uniform stylistic approach. Even a great sculptor like Melchiorre Cafà, who never actually worked with Bernini himself, would draw inspiration from the master for his masterpiece, the *Ecstasy of St Catherine of Siena*, a marble altarpiece in the church of Santa Caterina a Magnanapoli executed between 1660-65. The artist, who was Maltese in origin, moved to Rome after 1658 and entered the workshop of Ercole Ferrata. He soon proved to be an accomplished sculptor and at his death in 1667 following an accident at work, he left many uncompleted works and deep regret for the loss of a great artist. In his relief depicting the *Ecstasy of St Catherine of Siena*, Cafà shows that he has fully absorbed Bernini's language in the scenographic appearance produced by the saint's white marble figure standing out against the polychrome marble background, in the extremely touching and moving effect created by the subtle upward movement of the figure, in the intensely devout and ecstatic expression on her face, and in the great technical skill revealed by the soft rich folds of her drapery.

Antonio Raggi (1624-1686) was Bernini's favourite pupil and was involved in most of the great sculptor's projects. He interpreted Bernini's style very sensitively, especially the dynamic movement of his art, infusing it with a grace and tenderness that revealed his awareness of the classicising movement that was now spreading throughout the field of painting as well as sculpture. After coming to Rome in 1643 he spent a short period of apprenticeship with Algardi before entering Bernini's workshop, where he worked for the rest of his life. In 1649, shortly after beginning work on the marble decoration of the nave of St Peter's, the master tasked him with executing the altar in the Alaleona chapel in the church of Santi Domenico e Sisto to Bernini's design: the *Noli me tangere* episode is portrayed by means of two splendid figures of Christ and Mary Magdalene placed on the centre of the altar against a painted background, framed by four columns reaching to the ceiling of the chapel, surmounted by the figure of an angel and flooded with light. Both figures are wrapped in rich draperies, which, in the case of Mary Magdalene, in particular, form a succession of deep folds underlining her kneeling position. Raggi gives us a foretaste of his personal artistic approach in the drapery, undoubtedly inspired by Bernini's manner, which plays a key role in underlining the expressiveness and composition of the piece, and in the figures distinguished by gentle attitudes. His career was intensely busy and Bernini was to reserve a conspicuous and important part of every project for him. Raggio took part in the restoration of the nave of Santa Maria del Popolo (1655-57), carved the *St Bernardino* in the Chigi Chapel in Santa Maria della Pace (1657), participated in the work on the Cathedra in St Peter's, executed the relief for the church of Sant'Agnese in Agone depicting the *Death of St Cecilia* (1662), partecipated in the decorative scheme of the church of Sant'Andrea al Qurinale (1662-65), sculpted the *Baptism of Christ* for the altar of the church of San Giovanni dei Fiorentini (1665-69), executed the *Angel with the Column* for the Ponte Sant'Angelo (1668-70), and, in 1672-79, he was among the leading artists carrying out the stuccowork in the church of the Gesù in one of the most important decorative programmes of the time.

Bernini had no rivals, he was the most sought-after and esteemed artist of the period and his fame had now reached other European countries north of the Alps. His incredible contribution to sculpture resulted in a flood of commissions for portraits, relief altarpieces to replace the more traditional painted works along with altars, chapels and funerary monuments. This favoured the emergence of numerous sculptors, who flourished in the powerful shade of the great master, as well as attracting flocks of foreign artists, who travelled to Rome to complete their artistic training and in the hope of participating in one of the many construction sites, artists such as the French painter Pierre Puget, the English sculptor Nicholas Stone and the Austrian Balthasar Permoser, who helped diffuse Bernini's influence in their countries of origin.

Fig. 43 Ercole Ferrata, *St Agnes* (1660) Rome, Church of Sant'Agnese in Agone.

The main protagonists of this fortunate season in Rome were Ercole Ferrata, Antonio Raggi, Melchiorre Cafà, Lazzaro Morelli, Francesco Aprile, Domenico Guidi, Paolo Naldini, Jacopo Antonio, Cosimo Fancelli, and Giovanni Antonio Mari.

One of the most important sculptural undertakings of these years was the decoration of the church of Sant'Agnese in Agone. After the completion of the *Fountain of the Four Rivers* in the context of the schemes intended to give Piazza Navona a more splendid and sumptuous appearance, Innocent X decided to rebuild the small church dedicated to St Agnes and to transform it into a family chapel holding the martyr's remains. The interior is richly decorated with marble and stucco reliefs transforming it into a monument to sculpture. Large altarpieces (Fig. 41) placed above the three altars and in the niches in the four piers supporting the dome alternate with statues: going anti-clockwise, they are the *Death of St Alexius* by Francesco Rossi (1660-63), *St Agnes* (Fig. 43;1660) by Ercole Ferrata, the *Martyrdom of St Emerentiana* (Fig. 42) by Ercole Ferrata (the top section of which was completed by Leonardo Retti in the early 18th century), the *Holy Family* by Domenico Guidi (1677-83), the *Death of St Cecilia* by Antonio Raggi (1662-66), *St Sebastian* by Pietro Paolo Campi (1719), and the *Martyrdom of St Eustace* by Melchiorre Cafà (1669, completed by Ercole Ferrata).

Comparing the altarpieces by Ferrata and Raggi allows us to examine the different personal approaches adopted by the two artists in interpreting Bernini's style: Ferrata's altarpiece has a clear layout in which the figures, reduced to the minimum in accordance with the fundamental principles of the theories of Classicism, are distinguished by their different gestures and expressions, while the lower

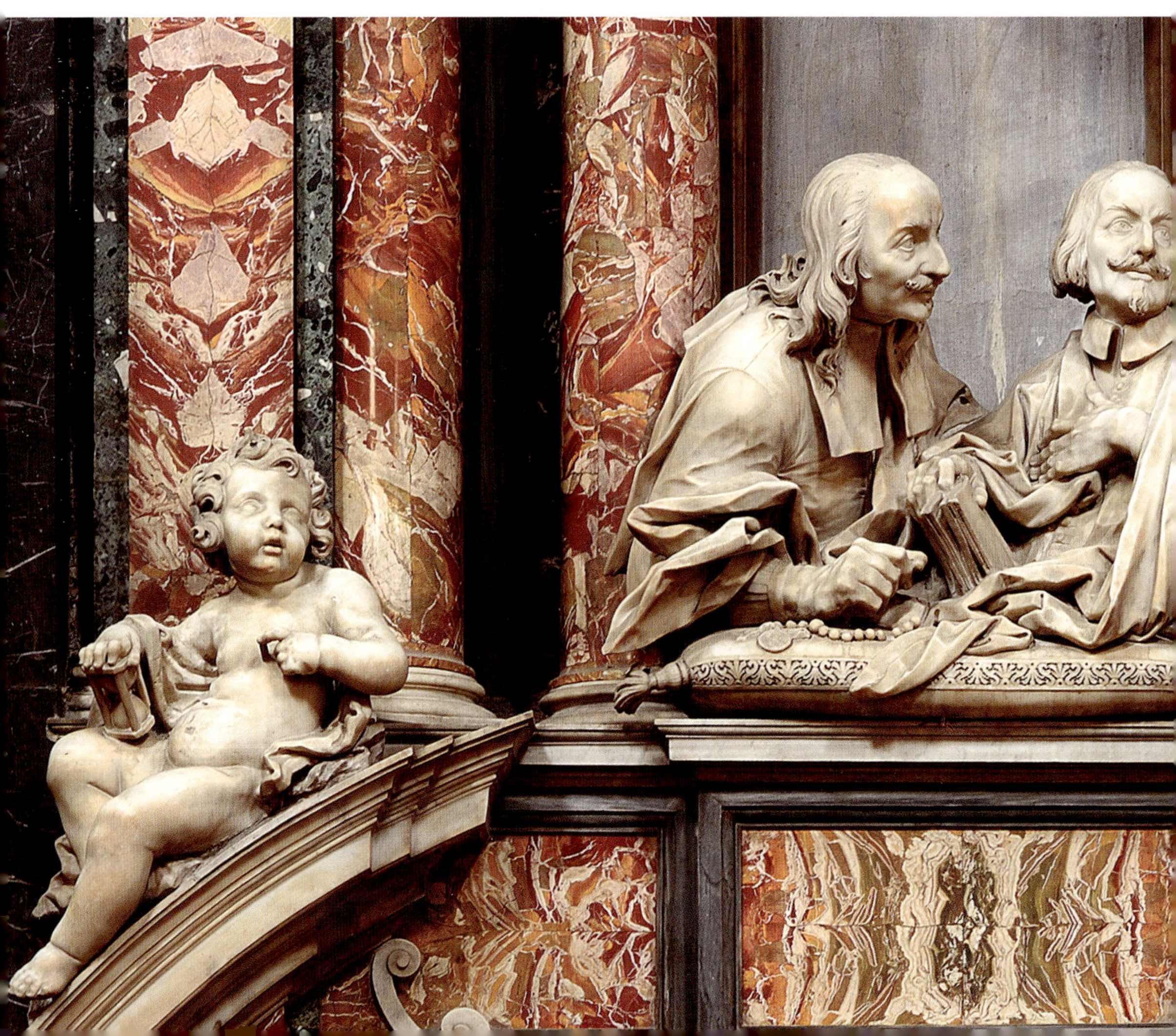

part of Raggi's altarpiece has an excited clamorous crowd whose confused movements betray the strong emotions aroused by the death of the saint; elongated figures with graceful measured movements represent a distinctive feature of his work.

Ercole Ferrata's statue of *St Agnes* (Fig. 43) is considered to be his masterpiece: his depiction of the saint – shown in the moment of her martydom surrounded by the flames that she quenches by the power of her profound faith, with a devout gaze and arms flung open wide – follows the path laid down by Bernini in creating his *St Bibiana* in terms of the strong emotional charge and intensely expressive face, but adopts a more measured language inspired by Algardi's manner for the gown falling simply along her body, even though the short mantle flutters in the wind, recalling so many of Bernini's statues, like St *Longinus*. Ferrata, a Lombard artist who went to Rome in 1647, was a prominent figure on the Roman artistic scene, not just because of his collaboration in so many of Bernini's undertakings, like the decoration of the nave of the basilica of St Peter and the nave of Santa Maria del Popolo, the Cathedra, the Scala Regia, the Ponte Sant'Angelo, to mention only the most important projects, but also because of the prestigious commissions awarded to him in person, which allowed him to set up his own, extremely busy workshop, which would turn out numerous artists including Melchiorre Cafà, Mazzuoli, Rusconi.

Other large-scale undertakings such as the *Ponte Sant'Angelo* and the church of Gesù e Maria (Fig. 44) confirm that even in the seventh and eighth decades of the 17th century, Bernini's style and manner continued to exercise an absolute hegemony upon the language used by sculptors and painters of the time.

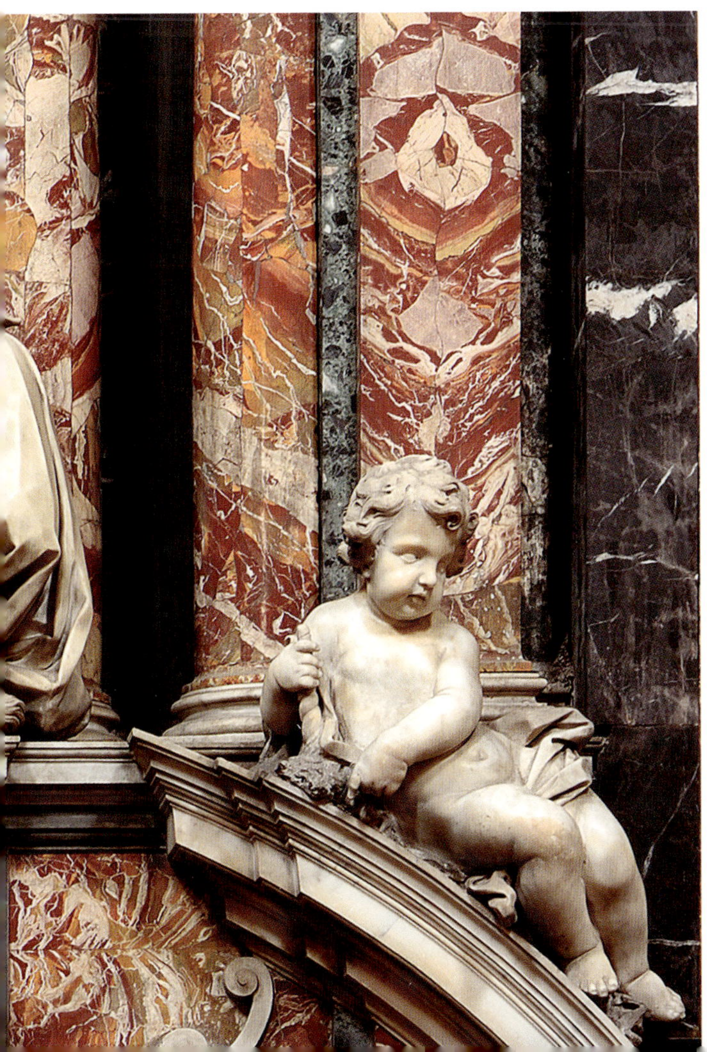

Fig. 44 Lorenzo Ottoni, *Funerary Monument of Ercole and Giovanni Luigi Bolognetti* (c. 1684), Rome, Church of Gesù e Maria.

TIMELINES

1598
Gian Lorenzo Bernini is born in Naples. His father, Pietro Bernini, a sculptor originally from Florence, had moved to the city to work at the Certosa di San Martino.

1606
Gian Lorenzo Bernini arrives in Rome, accompanying his father who has been called by Paul V to carry out the decorations of the Pauline Chapel in Santa Maria Maggiore. The relief depicting the *Assumption of Mary*, originally intended for the chapel façade, is considered his masterpiece.

1609-1618
Cardinal Maffeo Barberini and his brother Carlo erect their family chapel in the church of Sant'Andrea della Valle, commissioning four statues, *St Martha, St John the Baptist, St John the Evangelist, St Mary Magdalen,* by Francesco Mochi, Pietro Bernini, Ambrogio Buonvicino and Cristoforo Stati, respectively. The young Bernini partecipates in the work alongside his father, executing a pair of putti for the pediment of the right wall (1618).

1615
An extremely young Bernini makes his debut as a sculptor by carving the small sculpture group depicting the *Goat Amalthea*, now in the Galleria Borghese. Some scholars even date the work to 1609.

1617
Cardinale Maffeo Barberini commissions the young sculptor to carry out a *St Sebastian*, now in the Museo de Arte Thyssen Bornemisza in Madrid.

1618-1625
Cardinal Scipione Borghese commissions Gian Lorenzo Bernini to execute three sculpture groups: *Aeneas and Anchises, Rape of Persephone, Apollo and Daphne*, all still *in situ* in the Galleria Borghese.

1621
Gregory XV is raised to the papal chair and bestows the title of knight or "cavaliere" on Bernini.

1623
Maffeo Barberini is elected pope and takes the name Urban VIII.

1623-1624
Bernini executes the sculpture of *St Bibiana* (Church of St Bibiana) and the *Portrait of Cardinal Bellarmino* (Church of the Gesù). Bernini creates the sculpture of *David* for Cardinal Alessandro Peretti Montalto. Following the sudden death of the prelate, Cardinal Scipione Borghese obtains the sculpture, which is now also in the Galleria Borghese.

1624-1633
The pope begins preparations for the 1625 Jubilee and charges Gian Lorenzo Bernini with creating a covering for the tomb of St Peter in the Vatican basilica, the *Baldacchino*. A whole retinue of Bernini's pupils and collaborators, including Francesco Borromini, work on the mighty 28.5-metre-high gilt-bronze and bronze structure, which is inaugurated on 29 June 1633.

1626
Giuliano Finelli, one of Bernini's close collaborators, executes the *Portrait of Maria Barberini Duglioli*, now in the Louvre.

1627-1647
In 1627 Bernini starts work on the *Funerary Monument to Urban VIII,* situated in the Vatican Basilica, which would only be completed in 1647. That very year he is appointed "Architetto di San Pietro", or chief architect of the basilica.

1629
Together with his father Pietro, Bernini executes the *Fountain of the Barcaccia* in the Piazza di Spagna.

1629-1633
François Duquesnoy sculpts the figure of *St Susanna*, his masterpiece, for the church of Santa Maria di Loreto.

C. 1630
Giuliano Finelli creates the *Bust of Cardinal Domenico Ginnasi*, now in the Galleria Borghese.

1632

Bernini executes the two versions of his *Portrait of Cardinale Scipione Borghese.*

1628-1639

After the completion of the *Baldacchino*, Pope Urban VIII wishes to complete the decorative scheme of the entire crossing area in the basilica of St Peter and yet again entrusts the project to Bernini. The artist creates a design dividing the massive piers into two sections: in the upper section, twisted columns originally part of the ciborium in the old medieval basilica frame the relics, while the lower sections contain four huge niches holding colossal statues: *St Longinus* executed by Bernini himself, *Veronica* by Francesco Mochi, *St Helena* by Andrea Bolgi and *St Andrew* by François Duquesnoy.

1637

Andrea Bolgi sculpts the *Bust of Laura Frangipane Mattei*, now in the church of San Francesco a Ripa.

1640

Alessandro Algardi executes the statue group depicting the *Ecstasy of St Philip Neri* for the church of Santa Maria in Vallicella.

C. 1640-1647

In his will Francesco Raymondi, Cleric of the Apostolic Chamber and Protonotary Apostolic, leaves orders for Bernini to create the decorative scheme for his chapel in San Pietro in Montorio, which is to include a marble altarpiece depicting *St Francis in Ecstasy* and sarcophagi in the side walls with portraits of the patron and his brother. The sculptures are carried out by Francesco Baratta and Andrea Bolgi.

1645

Algardi sculpts a relief with the *Meeting of Leo I and Attila* for the basilica of St Peter.

1647-1649

Between 1647 and 1649 Bernini sculpts the *Portrait of Innocent X* (Galleria Doria Pamphilj). Antonio Raggi receives a commission from Sister Maria Alaleona to create a sculpture group depicting the *Noli me tangere* for the Alaleona Chapel in the church of Santi Domenico e Sisto.

1647-1653

On behalf of the Cornaro family, Bernini designs the decorative scheme for their family chapel in Santa Maria della Vittoria, bringing about the complete fusion of the arts – architecture, sculpture and painting – into a highly scenographic whole. The sculpture group depicting *St Teresa and the Angel* placed on the altar uses light effects and different materials to bring the ecstatic vision of the saint to life.

1648-1651

On behalf of Innocent X, Bernini works with a group of collaborators to create the *Fountain of the Four Rivers* in Piazza Navona. This monument is one of Rome's most important landmarks.

1650

Bernini executes the *Bust of Francesco I d'Este.*

1655

Cardinal Fabio Chigi rises to the papal throne taking the name Alexander VII.

1655-1661

Bernini and his collaborators, Paolo Naldini, Lazzaro Morelli, Antonio Raggi, Giovanni Antonio Mari, Ercole Ferrata and Arrigo Giardè, execute the decoration of the nave and transept of the church of Santa Maria del Popolo. Bernini completes the Chigi Chapel in the same period.

1656-1673

Alexander VII charges Bernini with designing piazza di San Pietro in front of the Vatican basilica. The artist constructs a spacious piazza encircled by an imposing colonnade surmounted by statues of saints, which are approximately three metres high. This huge construction site, which would continue for several years, involves a whole retinue of artists including Lazzaro Morelli, Andrea Baratta, Francesco and Domenico Mari, Giovan Maria Rossi and Nicola Artusi.

1657-1666

Bernini and his collaborators execute the colossal scenographic machine dedicated to the *Cathedra Petri*, in the apse of the Vatican basilica. Cosimo Fancelli executes the bronze relief depicting the *Trinity* for the church of Santa Maria della Pace commissioned by Pope Alexander VII.

1660-1665
Melchiorre Cafà executes the relief with the *Ecstasy of St Catherine* for the church of Santa Caterina a Magnanapoli.

1660-1709
In 1660 Bernini begins the sculpture decorations for the church of Sant'Agnese in Agone. The most important reliefs include the *Martyrdom of St Emerentiana* by Ercole Ferrata and Leonardo Retti, *St Agnes in the Flames* by Ercole Ferrata and the *Death of St Cecilia* by Antonio Raggi.

1661
Bernini completes the decorations for the Chigi Chapel in Santa Maria del Popolo and executes the two marble statue groups depicting *Habakkuk and the Angel* and *Daniel in the Lions' Den.*

1662-1668
Bernini designs a chapel for Gabriele Fonseca, a physician of Portuguese origin, in the church of San Lorenzo in Lucina, executing a moving portrait of the patron. In 1662 Bernini also executes the statues of *St Jerome* and *Mary Magdalene* for the Chigi Chapel in the Duomo of Siena and designs the equestrian statue of *Emperor Constantine.*

1663-1666
While work is still underway on the colonnade of St Peter's, Bernini refurbishes the official entrance to the papal palace (*Scala Regia*) with a rich stucco decoration and sets up an equestrian statue of Constantine that he began in 1662.

1665
Bernini travels to Paris (25 April-October) where he will execute the *Portrait of Louis XIV.*

1665-1667
Melchiorre Cafà and Ercole Ferrata carry out the sculpture group depicting the *Alms of St Thomas of Villanova* for the church of Sant'Agostino. During those same years Ferrata executes the *Monument to Lelio Falconieri*, probably to the design of Francesco Borromini, for the church of San Giovanni dei Fiorentini.

1667-1671
Papa Clemente IX Rospigliosi commissions Bernini to create the decorative scheme for the Ponte Sant'Angelo consisting of ten statues of angels bearing the instruments of the Passion. The first two to be sculpted by the master so captivate the pope that he orders Bernini to protect them from exposure to the elements and to keep them in a safe place. The sculptures remain in the artist's studio until the 18th century when they will be taken to the church of Sant'Andrea delle Fratte. Bernini personally executes the second version of the *Angel with the Superscription of the Cross*; the other angels are carved by Antonio Raggi, Lazzaro Morelli, Girolamo Lucenti, Cosimo Fancelli, Ercole Ferrata, Domenico Guidi, Antonio Giorgetti and Paolo Naldini.

1671-1675
Cardinal Paluzzo Paluzzi Albertoni, nephew of Pope Clemente X, commissions Bernini to carry out the decoration of the Albertoni Chapel in San Francesco a Ripa.

1672
Gian Lorenzo Bernini and his collaborators begin work on the Altar of the Sacrament in St Peter's (completed in 1674). Antonio Raggi, Leonardo Retti, Giovanni Rinaldi and Michel Maille all participate in the execution of the vast complex stucco decoration scheme for the Church of the Gesù (completed in 1679).

1673
Domenico Guidi executes the *Tomb of Cardinal Lorenzo Imperiale*, Cleric of the Apostolic Chamber at the time of Urban VIII, in the Church of Sant'Agostino.

1679
Bernini executes his last sculpture (now lost and known only through copies) depicting the *Salvator Mundi* and bequeaths it to Queen Christina of Sweden.

C. 1680
Ercole Ferrata executes the *Monument to Monsignor Giulio del Corno* for the Church of Gesù e Maria.

1680
Bernini dies in Rome on 28 November and is buried with full honours beside the high altar of the Church of Santa Maria Maggiore.

BASIC BIBLIOGRAPHY

BACCHI A., *Scultura del '600 a Roma,* Milan 1996.

BACCHI A. – TUMIDEI S., *Bernini. La scultura in San Pietro,* Milan 1998.

BERNARDINI M. G., *L'estasi in Bernini e il sentimento religioso nel secolo XVII,* in *Bernini a Montecitorio. Ciclo di conferenze nel quarto centenario della nascita di Gian Lorenzo Bernini,* edited by M. G. Bernardini, Rome 2001, pp. 129-151.

BERNINI D., *Vita del Cavalier Gio. Lorenzo Bernini,* Rome 1713.

Bernini scultore. La nascita del barocco in casa Borghese, exhibition catalogue edited by A. Coliva and S. Schütze, Rome 1998.

COLIVA A., *Bernini scultore: la tecnica esecutiva,* Rome 2002.

FAGIOLO DELL'ARCO M., *Bernini, una introduzione al gran teatro del Barocco,* Rome 1967.

FAGIOLO DELL'ARCO M., *Un modello di cantiere berniniano. La fabbrica di San Tommaso da Villanova a Castel Gandolfo,* in *Bernini a Montecitorio. Ciclo di conferenze nel quarto centenario della nascita di Gian Lorenzo Bernini,* edited by M. G. Bernardini, Rome 2001, pp. 7-30.

FERRARI O. – PAPALDO S., *Le sculture del Seicento a Roma,* Rome 1999.

Gian Lorenzo Bernini. Regista del Barocco, exhibition catalogue edited by M. Fagiolo dell'Arco and M. G. Bernardini, Milan 1999.

Gian Lorenzo Bernini. Regista del Barocco. I restauri, edited by C. Strinati, M. G. Bernardini, Milan 1999.

I marmi vivi. Bernini e la nascita del ritratto barocco, exibition catalogue edited by A. Bacchi, T. Montanari, B. Paolozzi Strozzi, D. Zikos, Florence 2009.

L'Ariccia del Bernini, exhibition catalogue edited by M. Fagiolo dell'Arco and F. Petrucci, Rome 1998.

LAVIN I., *Bernini and the Unity of the Visual Arts,* Oxford University Press 1980.

MARTINELLI V., *Gian Lorenzo Bernini e la sua cerchia. Studi e contributi (1950-1990),* Naples 1994.

MONTAGU J., *Roman Baroque sculpture. The Industry of Art,* Yale University Press 1989.

MORELLO G., *Bernini e i lavori a San Pietro nel diario di Alessandro VII,* in *Bernini in Vaticano,* exhibition catalogue, Rome 1981, pp. 321-340.

NAVA CELLINI A., *La scultura del Seicento,* Turin 1982.

PREIMESBERGER R., *Il San Longino del Bernini in San Pietro in Vaticano: dal bozzetto alla statua,* in *Bernini a Montecitorio. Ciclo di conferenze nel quarto centenario della nascita di Gian Lorenzo Bernini,* edited by M. G. Bernardini, Rome 2001, pp. 95-112.

SCHLEGEL U., *Il giovane Bernini,* in *Bernini a Montecitorio. Ciclo di conferenze nel quarto centenario della nascita di Gian Lorenzo Bernini,* edited by M. G. Bernardini, Rome 2001, pp. 45-58.

SUTHERLAND HARRIS A., *La Cattedra di San Pietro in Vaticano: dall'idea alla realizzazione,* in *Bernini a Montecitorio. Ciclo di conferenze nel quarto centenario della nascita di Gian Lorenzo Bernini,* edited by M. G. Bernardini, Rome 2001, pp. 113-128.

WITTKOWER R., *Gian Lorenzo Bernini. The Sculptor of the Roman Baroque,* Phaidon Press 1981.

Printed in March 2014
by Miligraf S.r.l., Rome